A TIME
TO
BE FREE

A TIME
TO
BE FREE

Daily Meditations for
Enhancing Self-Esteem

By the Author of
A Day at a Time and
A New Day

BANTAM BOOKS
NEW YORK • TORONTO • LONDON • SYDNEY • AUCKLAND

A TIME TO BE FREE
A Bantam Book / January 1991

Library of Congress Cataloging-in-Publication Data

A Time to be free.
    p. cm.
    ISBN 0-553-35203-2
    1. Adult child abuse victims—Prayer-books and devotions—
English.
    2. Devotional calendars.
    BV4596.A25T55   1991
    242'.4—dc20   90-42007
                                                          CIP

Published simultaneously in the United States and Canada

Bantam Books are published by Bantam Books, a division of Bantam
Doubleday Dell Publishing Group, Inc. Its trademark, consisting of
the words "Bantam Books" and the portrayal of a rooster, is
Registered in U.S. Patent and Trademark Office and in other
countries. Marca Registrada. Bantam Books, 666 Fifth Avenue, New
York, New York 10103.

Contents

A TIME
TO
BE FREE

1

The Influences That Shape Us

How did I get here? Somebody pushed me. Somebody must have set me off in this direction and clusters of other hands must have touched themselves to the controls at various times, for I would not have picked this way for the world.

—JOSEPH HELLER

January 1

There comes a time when we are finally willing to open the door to a better life. We realize, deep down and often suddenly, that we can no longer continue on the same path. If we do, things will only become worse—*and we deserve better*.

If someone were to ask what triggered our moment of clarity, each of us would likely give a different answer. For some, the catalyst was unbearable emotional pain. For others, a brief conversation or glance in the mirror may have brought about an unexpected awakening.

Our first positive actions were similarly individual and varied. Some picked up the phone to seek professional help or contact a twelve-step program. Others confided their anguish and newfound resolve to a friend or relative. For many, the initial step was a heartfelt prayer to God.

What we didn't realize, when we took these actions, was that we would soon cross the threshold into a joyous new life. We had no idea that we were about to begin an incredibly exciting and enriching journey—one of self-discovery, self-renewal, and self-love.

THOUGHT FOR TODAY: A moment of clarity can be a turning point—from stagnation and resignation to joy and peace of mind.

The Influences That Shape Us

We didn't get out of bed one morning and suddenly find ourselves fearful, unhappy, alienated, addictive, or simply unable to cope. The seeds of our behavior, thinking patterns, and sense of self were sown long ago.

The fact is that most of us who grew up in dysfunctional families ended up as dysfunctional adults. Because we had developed little or no self-esteem, we experienced life as an endless rough road rutted with problems and pain.

We've come to realize that we built our self-image and many of our perceptions from the messages and reactions of those around us, especially our parents. The way we were treated, physically and emotionally, set the patterns for the way we ultimately treated ourselves and others.

If we were constantly abused, ridiculed, or manipulated with guilt, we grew up needy of approval, guilt-ridden, and hobbled with low self-esteem. Moreover, the fear we experienced as children followed us into adulthood—as did our inability to be trusting, loving, and responsible.

The most important realization of our new lives is this: Although we can't do anything to change yesterday, as much as we'd like to, we do have choices concerning the way we live today.

THOUGHT FOR TODAY: I can continue to be ruled by the voices of the past—or I can work toward changing my perceptions and actions today.

The Influences That Shape Us

January 3

As we progress in our recovery, we're gradually able to unearth and identify the realities of our formative years. By bringing to light the ways in which we were influenced and shaped in the past, we begin to understand our behavior and thinking today.

For some of us, the connection between past and present was at first elusive. The forms of abuse in our dysfunctional families were subtle. It was hard to see that the damage we carried was as real and crippling as that suffered by victims of physical and sexual abuse.

But over time our insight has deepened. We can see that there are many ways to frighten and intimidate children besides beating them. Those of us in households with overpowering, overpossessive, and overpermissive parents, for example, frequently became emotional cripples. Similarly, if we grew up haunted by the fear of abandonment, it became all but impossible to develop a sense of well-being and security.

No matter what form of abuse we suffered, we carried the damage into adulthood. Now it's up to us to continue the healing process, replenishing ourselves mentally, emotionally, and spiritually—a day at a time.

THOUGHT FOR TODAY: Emotional violence can be just as crippling as physical violence.

For years I steadfastly held to the belief that my background—the severe emotional abuse I endured as a child—made me completely unique.

One day a woman friend described her feelings about herself—feelings flowing directly from sexual abuse she had suffered in earlier years. I suddenly realized that neither of us was as unique as we might have thought. Our circumstances may have been poles apart, but our feelings of self-hatred were identical.

By following her example—learning to talk openly and honestly about my experiences—it became clear that we shared the same negative feelings, regardless of how we were mistreated.

We experienced the world as a battleground, expecting to be ambushed at any moment. We feared success as well as failure, closeness as well as rejection, life as well as death. We developed complicated schemes to keep others from getting close to us, hiding ourselves and our true feelings behind elaborate costumes and disguises.

When one of those old feelings takes charge occasionally, I remind myself that I am not unique in this regard—and never was. Hundreds of thousands of other people have successfully worked through similar feelings, going on to lead satisfying and productive lives.

THOUGHT FOR TODAY: When I concentrate on the differences rather than the similarities, I delay my recovery.

The Influences That Shape Us

January 5

It is frustratingly difficult to overcome the destructive messages of the past, as well as our predictable responses to them. Indeed, it often seems impossible. Building a positive self-image by ignoring or rerecording old tapes seems about as easy as draining the ocean with a paper cup.

In the past we had tried time and again to change, but had failed repeatedly. We may have been successful for a day, a week, or even longer, but at some point fell back into our old ways. Inevitably, when someone or something switched on a deeply grooved old tape, we listened, took it to heart, and reacted defensively.

Even when we approached the challenge with dogged determination and plenty of willingness, we still lacked faith in our ability to succeed.

While we assuredly must have willingness before change can occur, we no longer must rely solely on our own resources. The key to success, we've learned, is asking for God's help, putting our faith in His power rather than our own. That is when the most lasting and rewarding changes have taken place in our lives.

THOUGHT FOR TODAY: Determination and willingness are only part of the formula for change. The secret ingredient is God's power.

When we open the door to the past, it's important to be clear about our motives for doing so. Let's not forget that for many years we went back for the wrong reasons.

We may have gone back to dwell morbidly on childhood misfortunes, using them to excuse self-destructive life-styles as adults. We may have taken a sort of perverse pleasure in punishing ourselves with memories of pain and embarrassment. Many of us used the past to see ourselves as doomed victims of circumstances; our theme song became "poor me."

Today the past has become a constructive rather than destructive force in our lives. We open the door to seek awareness and understanding of the influences that shaped us. We gain insight into our present thought patterns and behavior and, in the process, are shown what actions we must take in order to move out of the problem and into the solution.

We were once convinced that our personal histories were liabilities—permanent barriers that would forever block our progress. Now we believe that just the opposite is true, that our past is one of our greatest assets in the pursuit of spiritual growth.

THOUGHT FOR TODAY: My willingness to return to the past—for the right reasons—can be the foundation for a serene and purposeful life.

The Influences That Shape Us

January 7

Affirmation

As I look at my past these days, I do so almost lovingly. I am grateful that a backward glance no longer evokes pain, guilt, and remorse, but instead reminds me of how far I have come.

I am grateful for the moment of clarity that led me from resignation and desperation to the threshold of a new life.

I am grateful that the echoes of the past no longer rule my life, tyrannizing me with irrational fears and the need for self-punishment.

I am grateful that I have stopped comparing my "war stories" with those of others, concentrating instead on our similar feelings and goals.

I am grateful that lasting and fulfilling changes have become possible through my trust in God's ability to bring them about.

I am grateful that I no longer indulge in self-pity when I look back, but instead see each past experience as necessary in bringing me toward the freedom and happiness I enjoy today.

THOUGHT FOR TODAY: With God's help in gaining new perspective, the past which once haunted and hobbled me can be the starting point for a new life.

The Influences That Shape Us 8

2

Alienation

Actually, the process of birth continues. The child begins to recognize outside objects, to react affectively, to grasp things and to coordinate his movements, to walk. But birth continues. The child learns to speak, it learns to know the use and function of things, it learns to relate itself to others, to avoid punishment and gain praise and liking. Slowly, the growing person learns to love, to develop reason, to look at the world objectively. He begins to develop his powers; to acquire a sense of identity, to overcome the seduction of his senses for the sake of an integrated life. . . . The whole life of the individual is nothing but the process of giving birth to himself; indeed, we should be fully born when we die—although it is the tragic fate of most individuals to die before they are born.

—ERICH FROMM

January 8

For as far back as I can remember, I felt different. No matter who I was with or where I was, I felt alienated, awkward, and afraid. Many of us share that feeling.

In many instances our problems at home caused us confusion and self-doubt. We were uncomfortable with other children and became isolated. Socializing was painful almost beyond endurance. As a result, we didn't develop the social skills necessary to help us feel that we belonged.

Even as adults, many of us were afraid to let others come close. Our distorted self-perception told us, "If they really knew you, they'd see how awful you are."

Gradually these days, because of a willingness to take risks, our feelings of apartness and alienation have begun to diminish. Perhaps the most important action we have taken is to share our feelings with others. We've learned that many people have similar feelings, and this knowledge alone has sharply reduced our sense of alienation. Moreover, we see that when we let others get close to us, they are usually willing to accept us for who we are.

The more we risk closeness with others, the better we feel about ourselves. And as our self-esteem rises, it's easier to feel "a part of" rather than "apart from."

THOUGHT FOR TODAY: I'm not alone in my sense of aloneness.

Alienation

A friend and I were out driving one day. When we passed her old high school, she recalled how painful those years had been for her. "I was terribly afraid of people and didn't know how to interact with the other kids," she said, "so I had no friends. I spent all my free time alone. During lunch I would hide in a stairwell."

My friend went on to recall her mixed emotions. She hated her fellow students, yet desperately longed to be part of the group. But she didn't make the effort because she was convinced that she would never be accepted. "They knew far more than I did about music, movies, politics, sex—everything. They spent time together and learned from each other, and they learned from their families."

She never had those opportunities because she was alienated from her peers and received virtually no attention, support, or guidance from her two alcoholic parents.

"Obviously I've come a long way," she said. "I have friends, and I'm able to be involved with people. But it's still difficult for me, and I have a tendency to isolate. So each day I make a point of reaching out to another person, trying to know them better or letting them get to know me better. It works—and it's really helped me a lot."

THOUGHT FOR TODAY: If you want to be close to others, take a risk—drop your guard and reach out.

Alienation

January 10

When we first heard someone talk about a "hole in the gut," we identified immediately. For most of our lives we had felt a deep emptiness and lack of purpose, as if a part of us were missing.

Without even realizing it, much of what we did in life was geared to filling that inner void. We sought to make ourselves complete by accumulating money and material possessions, by pursuing social prestige and professional recognition. Some of us responded to our *dis-ease* with various forms of compulsive behavior—such as overeating, drinking, and using drugs.

The more desperately we tried to fill ourselves, the emptier we felt. Some of us achieved great material success, only to feel more frustrated and alienated than ever.

It never occurred to us that our deprivation was of a spiritual nature. Although each of us became aware of this reality in a different way, we all discovered that what we sought could not be found in the material world. It was when we looked within ourselves and began a spiritual quest that we were able to finally find a true sense of purpose and wholeness.

THOUGHT FOR TODAY: The emptiness within cannot be filled by material pursuits, but by discovering our spiritual selves.

Alienation

There were times in early recovery when my sense of alienation was so intense that it seemed I had just arrived in a foreign country. I felt lost and out of place. It was as if I didn't understand the local language, customs, values, and morals.

The thing is, I was disconnected from the world and had been since childhood. Because I had been alienated from my self for so long, I had no real grasp of reality or even who I was. I knew very little about my wants and needs, what I liked or disliked, what was good or bad, what direction in life was right for me.

For a frenzied year or more, I did things, bought things, entered relationships, and made career choices which, from today's vantage point, were not in my best interest.

Looking back, I can see that the greatest challenge—and richest rewards—in those early months of recovery came from drawing closer to myself, and beginning to appreciate and care about the real me I had never known. Before long I experienced a new sense of belonging and "citizenship," and a secure awareness that I was finally in the right place and on the right path.

THOUGHT FOR TODAY: So long as I am alienated from my true self, the right choices are hard to make.

Alienation

January 12

Many of us who came from dysfunctional families learned that to reveal feelings or have opinions was to invite ridicule or punishment. It became as natural as breathing to deny or conceal what we felt or believed.

As a consequence we entered the adult world alienated from ourselves—out of touch with our wants, needs, thoughts, values, and feelings. The world within was undiscovered, unexplored, unlived. We were estranged from our own essence.

How did we begin to break free from that stultifying existence? We made self-discovery a primary goal. By sharing and writing about long-suppressed feelings, beliefs, and concerns, we were able to get to know ourselves.

In addition, we made an effort to identify our impressions and reactions to situations we faced each day. We explored our feelings as they related to the reality of the moment. And, as difficult as it was at first, we forced ourselves to make commitments, to take stands, and to express opinions.

Before long, we adventurously participated in life, instead of merely going through the motions. Our once-dreary world became vibrant and intriguing.

THOUGHT FOR TODAY: The inner search has no ending, but it leads to endless beginnings.

When we saw other people making progress in their lives, we wondered why we weren't getting anywhere. They were happily married, while we were going through our third agonizing divorce. They were getting promotions and raises, while we were trying to hang on to our fourth job in a year.

We've come to realize that a major cause of our difficulties was alienation—we were disconnected from others, from ourselves, and from God.

Because we were disconnected, we didn't fully learn from our experiences. So we ended up going through them over and over, never making any real progress. It was as if we had been sleepwalking through our own lives, awakening abruptly from time to time without knowing where we were.

Today our primary objective is to progress spiritually, striving to strengthen our connection with God and our fellows. We see each experience as an opportunity for growth. We try to gain new insights and learn new lessons from whatever is put in our path.

Because we try to do what's good and right, because things matter to us, because we care about ourselves and others—we really have begun to live.

THOUGHT FOR TODAY: It's only when we learn from what's been put in our path that we can move further along.

Alienation

January 14

Affirmation

Today I will focus on growing toward oneness with myself, other people, and my Creator.

Today I will acknowledge my feelings, thoughts, and opinions, affirming that they are a valued part of me, worthy of expression. I will draw closer to myself, with the goal of continued self-discovery.

Throughout the day I will be present and accounted for, making an effort to learn from everything that is in my path. I will try to increase my self-awareness by identifying and exploring my reactions to events and interactions as they unfold.

Today I will be willing to take the risks necessary to build partnerships. I will reach out not once, but as often as possible in order to get to know others, and to let them get to know me.

Today I will strive to strengthen the connection between my Higher Power and me, reaffirming that it is through spiritual growth rather than material pursuits that I can experience a true sense of purpose, wholeness, and belonging.

THOUGHT FOR TODAY: The move from alienation to fellowship is gradual, but achievable. There are actions I can take each day to further my progress.

3

Guilt

Guilt upon the conscience, like rust upon iron, both defiles and consumes it, gnawing and creeping into it, as that does which at last eats out the very heart and substance of the metal.

—ROBERT SOUTH

January 15

Guilt dies hard. No matter what its genesis—whether it is imposed by others or is self-imposed—we often needlessly carry the burden for years. Indeed, guilt has been one of the most destructive and unrelenting forces in our lives.

What happens when we hold on to guilt? What are some of the damaging effects? We are all familiar with the lingering depression and emptiness that accompany self-condemnation—the feeling that we've never done anything right and probably never will.

When we carry guilt, we're often angry at ourselves. And this fuels the self-loathing that has already been simmering away in so many of us. Not surprisingly, we're in constant turmoil because of such feelings. We're always on the defensive, and over time our self-esteem and confidence sink lower and lower.

Worst of all, guilt ties us to the past, trapping us in distorted echoes and memories as life passes us by.

Until now, we knew very little about guilt. We didn't know how to deal with it or get rid of it—we didn't even understand it. But today we're learning how to unburden ourselves. We're moving from the past into the present.

THOUGHT FOR TODAY: Guilt is corrosive. The longer we hold on to it, the more we're damaged.

When we were young, many of us felt responsible for the discord and trauma in our households. We believed it was somehow our fault when our parents fought, got drunk, were unhappy, or couldn't pay their bills. If they divorced each other or deserted us, we saw our "badness" as the cause.

Some of us even blamed ourselves for the sexual and physical abuse we received. We were convinced that our behavior had brought it on—we had "asked" for it. If we were constantly ridiculed and criticized, we felt we deserved that too—because we were stupid, inept, or just plain worthless.

The guilt we collect as children often remains with us for a long time. Even as adults we may feel that what happened in childhood was somehow our fault. And that misguided perception can have negative impacts on all our grown-up relationships, especially the one with ourselves.

When we finally realize that our guilt is without foundation and inappropriate, we take the first big step toward freeing ourselves from the past. As we progress in recovery, giving up illusions and seeing the past realistically, we learn to practice acceptance and forgiveness. And our burden of guilt grows ever lighter.

THOUGHT FOR TODAY: Does the discomfort I sometimes feel about my past have anything to do with residual and groundless guilt?

Guilt

"Last week my boss asked me to put off my vacation again," a friend told me. "I'd had reservations for months, and he knew it, but he asked me anyway. When I said no, he did his usual number and tried to make me feel guilty. And I did—but only for about fifteen minutes this time."

Like so many of us, my friend grew up manipulated and controlled by guilt. If he didn't behave, dress, or respond as his parents expected, they would bombard him with guilt-giving messages until he conformed. "Sometimes all it took was a deep sigh or a look of disappointment to make me give in," he said. "My mother was a master at that."

Not surprisingly, my friend's childhood conditioning carried over into adulthood. It took very little for him to feel guilty. It was all but impossible not to respond to manipulative "guilt-givers" such as his boss.

"I finally figured out that I no longer have to *accept* guilt," my friend explained. "I know I'm a good person and a good employee. I'm grounded in reality these days, so it takes a lot more than a sidelong glance or innuendo to throw me off balance."

THOUGHT FOR TODAY: My thoughts and actions today will be motivated not by guilt, but by knowledge of what is good and right for me.

When it comes to imposing guilt on myself, I do a better job than anyone. It's as if I'm walking around with a miniature courtroom in my head. In a split second I can become my own prosecutor, judge, and jury.

"You should be doing a better job," the prosecutor accuses, and the jury quickly condemns me to several hours of guilt. "You ought to be a better person," shouts the judge, and the jury returns with a verdict of self-condemnation.

The charges pile up until I am overwhelmed. I feel inadequate, incompetent, and worthless. But most of all, I feel *guilty*.

When this happens, I have to shake myself back to reality—back to the awareness that I alone am responsible for the false arrest, trumped-up charges, and cruel and unusual punishment.

The court is far less likely to convene and press charges, I find, when I watch my language—especially the language of my thoughts. I try not to be sucked in by my own negative brain chatter—the "shoulds," "oughts," and "musts." Moreover, I try to counteract self-punishing messages with nurturing ones that build my self-esteem.

THOUGHT FOR TODAY: When my mind sends me a derogatory message, I will counterattack with truth rather than succumb with guilt.

Guilt

January 19

Many of us still are weighed down with guilt for things we did in the past. It's certainly not wrong or inappropriate to feel guilty when our actions cause harm to others. What is unhealthy is to remain under a cloud of guilt for months or years without doing anything about it.

In my own case, even after I had been sober for a while, I continued to punish myself for hurtful acts I had committed when drinking. As a result, my emotional recovery lagged behind my physical recovery. Because I still perceived myself as the sick person I once had been, my self-esteem remained at rock bottom. Suffice it to say I was on shaky ground.

When we're ready to rid ourselves of lingering guilt and become free of the past, there are specific actions we can take to help us. We can write about and reveal—to ourselves, another person, and God— the nature of our wrongs. If we haven't yet done so, we can then make amends to those we harmed.

Finally, we can ask God for forgiveness and, equally important, we can try to forgive ourselves.

THOUGHT FOR TODAY: If I'm willing to take constructive actions, I can become free of lingering guilt.

As painful and destructive as guilt can be, why is it that some of us continue to accept it—or refuse to let it go—even after we know better? The reason, we've discovered, is that we're still getting something out of our guilt.

It's not that we consciously say, "I need to continue feeling guilty so I can reap some rewards." We're *unaware* that we want or expect a payoff.

When we're afraid or unwilling to make necessary changes in our life, for example, hanging on to guilt allows us to stay where we are. We don't have to take risks, we don't have to take action, we don't have to do anything.

Since the message of guilt is "I'm bad," feeling guilty enables us to feel sorry for ourselves. When we manipulatively express that self-pity to others, they usually give us sympathy and compliments.

Still another payoff is that we can sometimes please others and make them "right" by staying guilty. With some people, the more guilty we become, the better they like it.

Of course, all of these so-called payoffs diminish rather than enhance our self-esteem. Our goal these days is to eliminate guilt and work instead toward positive and lasting rewards.

THOUGHT FOR TODAY: There are no payoffs, only penalties when I hang on to guilt.

Guilt

Affirmation

I will seek lightness of spirit in my new life. With God as my source of wisdom and strength, I will become free of limiting thoughts and behavior.

I will remain aware that much of my lingering guilt is groundless, and damaging to my spiritual being.

As I release my burden of guilt, the healing process will accelerate. Depression, emptiness, and self-condemnation—the handmaidens of my guilt—will be replaced by self-confidence and peace of mind.

The decisions and choices I make today will flow from realistic assessments of what is good and right. I will not allow myself to be manipulated or motivated by guilt.

If I am still weighed down with guilt for past acts, I will make amends so that I can move forward. God has long since forgiven me, and it is now time for me to forgive myself.

Through my prayers and meditation, I will affirm that God is a loving force in my life. He does not condemn me, but wants me to be happy, joyous, and free.

THOUGHT FOR TODAY: I will travel light on my spiritual journey, without the baggage of guilt.

4

Surrender

I don't know who—or what—put the question, I don't know when it was put. I don't even remember answering. But at some moment I did answer "Yes" to Someone or something. And from that hour I was certain that existence is meaningful and that, therefore, my life, in self-surrender, had a goal.

—DAG HAMMARSKJÖLD

January 22

When we hear the word *surrender*, certain images come automatically to mind: a line of bedraggled and weaponless soldiers marching toward a prisoner-of-war camp; a prizefight manager throwing in the towel; someone waving a white flag. It's hard not to think of surrender as something tragic and wholly negative. We've been culturally conditioned from childhood to keep fighting, no matter what. We abhor the idea of giving up.

For all of these reasons, the spiritual principle of surrender, as essential as it is to rebirth and renewal, can be a difficult one to grasp and put into practice.

In spiritual terms, surrender is not only an admission of defeat but, more importantly, the recognition at gut level that we have only limited power to bring about change. It is the acknowledgment that we cannot, by force of will alone, rid ourselves of character defects, obsessions, addictions, and self-bondage in its many forms.

Surrender, as we've come to understand it, is also the admission that we need help from a Power greater than ourselves. As we begin to apply this concept in our everyday lives, it takes on an entirely different meaning: winning rather than losing.

THOUGHT FOR TODAY: When I surrender, I allow God to enter my life and bring about change.

We don't just glance at our wristwatch and decide it's time to surrender. We have to hit bottom first—physically, emotionally, or spiritually. What brings us to that point is of course a highly individual matter, varying from one person and situation to the next.

In the case of addiction, the "bottom" can range from minor indebtedness to a suicide attempt. Similarly, if the difficulty stems from a destructive personal relationship, the bottom can as easily be "one argument too many" as a violent confrontation.

Some people speak of a "moment of clarity," during which they become suddenly and sharply aware of the destructiveness of a particular attitude or behavior pattern. Whatever the personal experience, hitting bottom and then surrendering usually involves the heartfelt admission that one can't go on in the same way for one more minute. It usually also leads one to seek help.

From that standpoint, a spiritual surrender is far more a beginning than it is an ending. It can bring a great sense of relief, while setting the stage for the necessary changes ahead. It can motivate us to take those actions that are within our power, and to turn the rest over to God.

THOUGHT FOR TODAY: I can get off the train at any stop. I don't have to go to the end of the line before I surrender.

Surrender

January 24

Two days in my life stand out sharply in memory. Both were marked by pivotal surrenders. On neither occasion did I fully realize what was taking place, yet from each of those days forward nothing was ever again the same.

The first surrender concerned my alcoholism. On that day I conceded to my deepest self that I had been utterly defeated by the bottle—and I sought help. Had I not made that first surrender, which saved my life and precipitated my recovery, the second surrender could not have occurred . . . .

Even after five years of sobriety, I continued to have serious living problems which stemmed from my dysfunctional upbringing. Practically from the day I got sober, I had struggled to "fix" my parents and our antagonistic relationship, hoping that in the process I could somehow undo the emotional damage that had been done to me.

The second surrender came on a day when I suddenly realized that my struggles would remain forever unsuccessful—that I was totally powerless over my parents and all that had occurred between us. On that day I admitted defeat, conceded that the emotional damage I had suffered was far too serious to handle on my own, and again sought help.

THOUGHT FOR TODAY: I am grateful that help was available when I finally surrendered.

When we finally gave up and admitted that our lives were unmanageable, it wasn't long before many things began to change for the better. We weren't alone anymore, and we could see that it was actually possible to get well. "That's that," we thought.

As for the rest of our problems, we decided we could handle them just fine on our own. While we had readily surrendered and accepted rescue from those dire emotional straits, we certainly didn't think the same thing was necessary for anything else.

We couldn't have been more wrong. It turned out we were just as powerless over our seemingly minor problems as we were the critical ones. Since that time, the spiritual principle of surrender has become an oft-used and invaluable tool in our lives. In fact, it sometimes seems that recovery is a series of surrenders.

We frequently find it necessary, for example, to surrender our will in favor of God's will. We surrender character defects, destructive relationships, illnesses, obsessions, disappointments—whatever it is we've been fighting to no avail. And sometimes, in order to truly accept our powerlessness and move forward, we make the same surrender over and over again.

THOUGHT FOR TODAY: The problem need not be life-threatening or even major for me to surrender—*and win*.

Surrender

January 26

"When I can still smile after the kind of day I had today, that's when I know I've really changed," my friend said proudly. "Someone overscheduled surgery, one of the other O.R. nurses called in sick, and on top of that we had an equipment failure."

My friend told me that not long ago she would have made herself crazy in that kind of situation. She would have gotten angry and stayed angry, would have created a tremendous amount of stress for herself, and would have felt that it was somehow her responsibility to get everything back on track.

What she did instead was try to stay in the now, concentrating on what was in front of her. She made a clear-minded decision not to complain, and not to worry about things that didn't concern her.

"I'm beginning to really get in touch with my powerlessness," she explained. "That's what happened today. I stopped fighting everything and everybody. I reminded myself that I was powerless over the surgery schedule, the equipment, and the other nurses. And when I did that, I immediately felt calm inside."

THOUGHT FOR TODAY: When I stop fighting and accept my powerlessness, I experience inner peace.

I know quite a bit about surrender. I've witnessed and experienced its positive impact on many occasions and in all kinds of situations. As far as I'm concerned, some form of surrender has to take place before true inner change can occur.

Given all that prior knowledge and conviction, you would think I'd apply this spiritual tool without hesitation when troubled by an obsession, a health or relationship problem, or a reemerging character defect.

Unfortunately, that's not what usually happens. Surrender is rarely my initial inclination, even though it's invariably what I end up doing. All too often, I first have to back myself into a corner by trying to think my way out, will my way out, or fight my way out. In the process I usually make myself and those around me miserable.

It's hard to say exactly why I resist surrendering. No doubt my recalcitrance stems from die-hard pride, self-will, or just plain stubbornness.

In all fairness, however, I don't hold out anywhere nearly as long as I used to. Thankfully, I'm becoming less willful as time goes on, and my tolerance for pain and frustration is steadily decreasing.

THOUGHT FOR TODAY: Am I still using my best resource as my last resort?

January 28

Affirmation

The paradox of strength in surrender has become a comforting reality in my life. When I give up my will in favor of God's will, I am at my best. As illogical as it may sound in a world where the drive for power is pervasive, I have discovered joy in powerlessness.

For a long time the principle of powerlessness was a difficult one to grasp. But through trial as well as necessity, it has proved to be a significant force for change and growth. When I surrender and admit my powerlessness, I allow the power of God to enter my life and bring about change.

I can surrender at any time; I need not wait until the bitter end. I can surrender anywhere; I need not find a special place. I can surrender anything; I need not reserve this trenchant tool for calamitous events.

When I admit my powerlessness over people, places, and things, my unwarranted sense of responsibility is lifted. Almost immediately I experience incredible relief.

My admission of defeat is not an ending, but a beginning. I am provided with the impetus to take actions within my capability, and to turn over to God those that are His.

THOUGHT FOR TODAY: There is joy in powerlessness.

5

Fear

My apprehensions come in crowds;
I dread the rustling of the grass;
The very shadows of the clouds
Have power to shake me as they pass:
I question things and do not find
One that will answer to my mind,
And all the world appears unkind.

—WILLIAM WORDSWORTH

January 29

For most of our lives, fear was our constant companion. It tyrannized and almost destroyed us. Hardly an hour passed when fear didn't cause us pain, panic, or even paralysis.

We experienced the world as a forbidding and sometimes terrifying place. We were afraid to be alone—or with other people. We were frightened of our parents and our teachers—authority of any kind. We feared responsibility, commitment, rejection, inadequacy, and exposure.

Besides being afraid of specific things such as the telephone or meeting someone new, we were afraid of things that weren't there—possibilities that could hardly be put into words.

Thankfully, we became sick and tired of living that way. We refused to be tyrannized any longer, and started taking actions to confront and overcome our fears. Confiding in other people brought us identification, support, and solutions.

Little by little we learned to walk through our fears—not with resignation and the expectation of pain, but with courage born of faith in God and a desire to change and be free.

THOUGHT FOR TODAY: With openness, action, and faith I can overthrow the dictatorship of fear.

Because the bottom fell out of our lives so often when we were young, we grew up riddled with self-centered fear. We were forever afraid that we would lose something we had, or not get something we wanted.

We have since learned that this deep-seated soul-sickness can trigger many of our other character defects—including anger, jealousy, envy, greed, closed-mindedness, intolerance, and unkindness.

Our fear of abandonment may cause us to become jealous or possessive of a boyfriend, girlfriend, or spouse. Our fear that we won't meet a deadline may cause us to lash out impatiently at a hardworking employee.

Similarly, we may become painfully envious of a friend's promotion—out of fear that *our* talents won't ever be acknowledged. Or we may remain closed-minded to new ideas—once again, because we're afraid of losing something we have, or of not getting something we want.

Today when we're having trouble with a character defect, the first thing we do is search for hidden fears. By tackling this oft-disguised emotion head on, we can avoid potentially destructive behavior and concentrate on what's really bothering us.

THOUGHT FOR TODAY: Do I avoid dealing with self-centered fear by disguising it with more "acceptable" emotions?

Fear

"My fear of people was tormenting enough," a friend told me one evening, "but the ways I compensated made it even worse. For instance, I was so afraid of being rejected that I hardly ever made an effort to get to know anyone new."

"Yeah, I know what you mean," I said. "One of my biggest fears was being belittled, so I protected myself with arrogance and one-upmanship."

"Confrontation was a big one for me," she said. "I did whatever I could to avoid it—not only backing down, but totally compromising my values and integrity."

"I did that too," I remembered. "But my ultimate fear was of people getting close. So I went out of my way to destroy relationships before they could get off the ground."

"How about this for pathetic," my friend said. "My worst fear was that other people would know that I was afraid."

We both started laughing. Then I said, "How did we get from there to here?"

"It took plenty of work to raise my self-esteem," she said seriously. "I had to bite the bullet and put myself on the line. That meant concentrating a lot less on what others thought of me, and a lot more on what I thought of myself."

THOUGHT FOR TODAY: I will not let my fear of people cause me to eclipse my real self.

When it was first suggested that I "replace fear with faith," it seemed that my problems were being trivialized or dismissed. The phrase sounded like it had come straight off a bumper sticker.

There soon came a time, however, when an automobile accident—and the need for emergency surgery—caused such overpowering fear that I became more than willing to try the advice that had once sounded so trite. I put aside my skepticism and asked for God's help. To my amazement, my fear lessened dramatically.

That's when I began to realize that my friends had supplied me with a practical and extremely effective tool for overcoming fear in all areas of my life. Through subsequent experiences, I learned that whenever I am afraid, I can find courage and strength by remembering that I am not alone—that God is always at my side to protect and care for me.

I know today that no fear is too small, too large, or too irrational for God's concern and involvement. Each time I turn to Him when I am afraid or insecure, my faith is strengthened.

THOUGHT FOR TODAY: I will replace my fear with faith that God is always present, offering direction and strength in all situations and circumstances.

Fear

February 2

Fearing the worst—we've lived that way for so long that we do it automatically. Instead of concentrating on what *is*, we focus fearfully on what could be or might be. Our thoughts and conversations frequently overflow with predictions of disaster: "They won't like me . . ." "It's going to get turned down . . ." "It's probably cancer . . . ."

If we have come from a dysfunctional family, perhaps we've remained locked in that childhood frame of reference: We could never count on anything, and never knew what to expect. But that was a long time ago. When we continue to project negatively on the landscape of the future, we take all the joy out of the here and now.

How can we put an end to this lifelong tendency? How can we stop our imaginations from running wild?

For one thing, we can try to ground ourselves in reality when phantom fears begin to haunt us. We can talk to ourselves as we would to a friend, reviewing only the facts, in a logical and supportive way. Most important, we can reaffirm the fundamental truth that God can and will continue to take care of us, no matter what.

THOUGHT FOR TODAY: If fears begin to cloud my day, I will focus on the facts rather than on the fiction.

More often than not these days, we do things for the right reasons—out of self-respect and love. But that wasn't always the case. For many years we were motivated by fear. Fear was our primary source of energy and action.

Because of our low self-esteem, we lived defensively. Many of our most important choices were made to *avoid* feelings of anxiety, guilt, and self-doubt—rather than to *experience* enjoyment and fulfillment.

We sought relationships, for example, not because of a true desire to give and receive love, but because we were afraid of being alone. We worked feverishly at our jobs, not for personal satisfaction or career advancement, but to avoid the fear of financial insecurity. We took care of our responsibilities, not out of pride, but because we feared the consequences of not taking care of them.

When low self-esteem compels us to act out of fear, we of course end up feeling even worse about ourselves. On the other hand, when our motives are good and right, we gain self-respect, self-confidence, and real satisfaction.

THOUGHT FOR TODAY: My choices and actions today will be motivated by a desire to enjoy life, rather than by a need to avoid the anxiety of living.

Fear

February 4

Affirmation

Now that I have begun to experience freedom from fear, my dark and limited world has brightened and expanded. I look forward enthusiastically to the exciting opportunities that lie ahead.

I am grateful that my thoughts and actions today are motivated by a thirst for freedom and fulfillment, and are no longer fueled by fear.

I can become free of damaging behavior such as impatience, anger, and jealousy by unearthing and dealing with the hidden fears that often activate my character defects.

Each time I summon the courage and faith to walk through fear, its power will diminish. With this knowledge and the expectation of ever-greater freedom, I can continue to confront and conquer my fears.

As the stranglehold of fear loosens, I am able to confide in others at deeper levels. As a result I become open to further insights and solutions to our common problem.

When new fears arise or old ones resurface, I can find reassurance and courage by turning to God. No matter what form my fears take—no matter how overwhelming or elusive they seem—He will always be there for me.

THOUGHT FOR TODAY: Faith is the key that unlocks the shackles of fear.

6

Addiction

I do not believe that sheer suffering teaches. If suffering alone taught, all the world would be wise, since everyone suffers. To suffering must be added mourning, understanding, patience, love, openness and the willingness to remain vulnerable.

—ANNE MORROW LINDBERGH

February 5

There were times, growing up, when we wondered why we had been brought into the world—and wished that we hadn't been. To some of us, home life was a nightmare of violence, broken promises, and secret terrors. For others, the worst pain came from aloneness; nobody was there for us, nobody cared about us.

Then we found a way out—a magical solution to our problems. Perhaps we found it early, when we were still preteens. Maybe we discovered it during adolescence, or later, as young adults. In any case, it gave us our first real sense of well-being. It made us feel that we finally belonged. It enabled us to feel comfortable, to *be somebody*. It took away the pain and helped us not to care as much. We found our addictions.

We escaped and found solace in alcohol, drugs, and food. We carved identities for ourselves and found love in sex and in one relationship after another. We became invulnerable and found respect through power over others. And we thought we could go on like that forever.

THOUGHT FOR TODAY: I am deeply grateful that my serenity and sense of belonging comes from within, rather than from addictive substances and behavior.

February 6

We turned to drugs, alcohol, food, and compulsive behavior as a way out of pain and unhappiness. It worked for a while, in some cases for a long while. But inevitably we crossed an invisible line into addiction. What had once seemed to be the solution was now the primary problem.

Ironically, many of us ended up in a nightmare existence even worse than the one we had tried to leave behind. We caused injury and heartache not only to ourselves, but to those around us. We ruined our health, we compromised our values and morals, we accumulated enormous burdens of shame and guilt. We carried on the family tradition.

When we hit bottom and threw in the towel, it was a blessing to finally admit that we were addicts, alcoholics, or compulsive overeaters. What a relief to discover that we were not alone, that there were places we could go for help, that there were solutions to our problems and guidelines for recovery. We were finally home.

THOUGHT FOR TODAY: My addictions stopped working for me long ago. I will give up any lingering reservations I may have about that reality.

Addiction

February 7

Toward the end, when my addictions were at their worst, I just knew that everything would be all right if only I could quit. The problems I'd been having in relationships would vanish. Things would turn around financially. I would automatically feel good and be happy.

In the early days of my recovery, it seemed that those hopes had become reality. But the temporary respite from my problems didn't last. Although I stayed clean and sober, my life soon became almost as unmanageable as before. I fought with my family; I had difficulty working; I was depressed, angry, and fearful.

What I didn't realize was that my addictions were but symptoms of an underlying living problem. When I gave up my chemical and behavioral dependencies, I not only was left with the same problems I started with years earlier, I had accumulated a painful array of new ones.

To recover in the broader sense, I was told, I would have to become rigorously self-honest. I would have to discover and discard the attitudes, perceptions, and personality traits causing my difficulties. I would have to stop blaming others and start taking responsibility. I would have to apply new tools and solutions to my living problems.

THOUGHT FOR TODAY: Now that I have unmasked my real problem—my living problem—I can begin to heal from the inside.

Growing up in dysfunctional homes, many of us had to depend on ourselves because we couldn't depend on anyone else. At an early age we developed various survival techniques such as secretiveness, self-control, and self-reliance. That's how we got by most of the time.

Later on, we expected that this same approach would work with our addictions. But when we tried to quit by using willpower and self-control, we failed dismally and repeatedly. Eventually we learned that we couldn't do it ourselves. Only when we admitted complete defeat and sought help from a Power greater than ourselves were we able to make a start in recovery.

We have come to be grateful for our addictions, strange as it may sound, because they led us to faith and trust in a Higher Power. Despite the pain and suffering of the past, our addictions and subsequent recovery have given us a new way to live.

We no longer have to depend only on ourselves for wisdom and strength in overcoming adversity. We have been offered spiritual tools which can be successfully applied in all areas of our lives.

THOUGHT FOR TODAY: I know from experience that God's limitless power is at my disposal. Why do I try to keep doing it myself?

Addiction

February 9

We absolutely had to have it, and we'd do anything to get it. We were addicted to approval.

We went into debt to acquire trappings designed to win compliments and recognition. We exaggerated, lied, and presented false images of ourselves. We ruined our health by working long hours and subjecting ourselves to stress and abuse. In short, we abdicated control of our lives to others and compromised our inner integrity.

Very often, we were successful; for the most part, people liked us. But of course we could never get enough. The more we got the more we needed. Many of us continually tortured ourselves trying to win over those one or two people—usually parents—whose approval had always been hard to come by.

Our recovery began with self-honesty, which gradually led to self-awareness. With help, we were able to understand what we were doing and to see how harmful it was.

These days, what matters most is gaining our *own* approval, rather than the approval of others. Regardless of the whims and wiles of friends, relatives, and employers, we try to remain true to ourselves in motive and deed.

THOUGHT FOR TODAY: Now that I am recovering from the addiction to approval, I am no longer dependent on others for my well-being.

Addiction

It was hard to believe that I hadn't taken a drink in 365 days. But it was true. As my family and many new friends applauded, I blew out the candle on my first "birthday" cake.

For more than a week I had planned and rehearsed what I was going to say. But when it came time to speak, the words stuck in my throat. I just stood there crying, more grateful than I had ever been in my life.

I was grateful to be alive and sober—to be moving around and in my right mind. I was grateful that the obsession to drink had been removed.

But that was just the beginning. The unquestionable miracle of my sobriety led me in time to deep faith in God. By following spiritual guidelines, it became possible not only to stay sober, but to live comfortably in my own skin and in the world for the very first time.

It became possible to let go of resentments I had carried for years. It became possible to be patient, tolerant, and caring. It became possible to give and receive love.

THOUGHT FOR TODAY: Now that I am clean and sober, the opportunities for growth are unlimited.

Addiction

February 11

Affirmation

Recovery brings with it an abundance of opportunities. Where I once had no choice but to focus desperately on my addictions, I am now free to approach each day with gratitude, enthusiasm, and the expectation of continued growth.

I have the opportunity to build friendships and experience fellowship based on deep caring and understanding. I have true partners who will always be there for me. My sense of belonging comes from within.

Initially, my only goal was to give up my chemical and behavioral dependencies. I had no idea that I would find a new way of life. In recovery I have been led to belief, faith, and growing trust in a God of my own understanding. I have been provided with spiritual solutions which enable me to live comfortably and harmoniously.

Along the way I have been given the opportunity to discover my real self. For the first time, I know where I stand in the world. I have a sense of purpose and direction that is right for me. Life today abounds with endless possibilities for excitement, wonder, and joy.

THOUGHT FOR TODAY: I will take time to reflect on the many gifts and opportunities in my new life.

7

Coming to Believe

What is there in man so worthy of honor and reverence as this, that he is capable of contemplating something higher than his own reason, more sublime than the whole universe—that Spirit which alone is self-subsistent, from which all truth proceeds, without which there is no truth?

—FRIEDRICH JACOBI

February 12

Coming to believe in a Power greater than ourselves—this occurrence has made a profound difference in our lives. Our new or redefined relationship with God not only has made recovery possible, but has brought about fundamental changes in our way of thinking, our outlook, and our behavior. Today, as the result, we are able to live happily, joyously, and freely.

For years we tried on our own to make new starts, to give up the addictions and obsessions that were destroying us. We wanted desperately to leave the past behind—to forgive and forget. We did the best we could to change the way we felt about ourselves and others.

While in some cases there was progress, we all reached a point from which we could advance no further. We saw that our personal resources were limited; clearly, we lacked the power to bring about deep and lasting change. It was then that we finally sought help. We came to believe that the power we lacked could be found in faith.

THOUGHT FOR TODAY: I need not struggle on my own. God's power is always available.

We saw indisputable evidence among our new friends that belief in a Higher Power had dramatically changed their lives for the better. That fact, along with our previous admission of powerlessness, convinced us that we couldn't build a successful new life without a solid spiritual foundation. Nevertheless, some of us remained leery of "the God thing."

We were afraid to venture forward in faith because we had been taught that God was judgmental and punishing. We may have lost faith because we felt He hadn't come through when we needed Him most. Perhaps we were atheists, or agnostics, or we'd been force-fed religion when we were younger.

When we expressed our concerns, our friends were empathetic and reassuring. They had been similarly apprehensive, they said; they too had initially focused on drawbacks, differences, and potential negatives. However, all they had to do to make a start, they told us, was to open their minds to the possibility that an all-powerful and loving God could and would help them if He were sought. And that's exactly what we did. We became open-minded, and the rest came to pass as promised.

THOUGHT FOR TODAY: We come to believe from different starting places and at different times. All we need is open-mindedness.

Coming to Believe

February 14

It was drummed into me as a boy that religion was "the opiate of the masses." I was taught that God was an invention designed to make people complacent and malleable through false hope. Those who spoke of God—whether from pulpits or in personal conversations—were liars and hypocrites.

It's little wonder that I was extremely uncomfortable with the spiritual concepts that were obviously so much a part of the recovery experience. When people talked about turning their wills and lives over to the care of God, I thought they had been brainwashed. When they expressed their gratitude to God, my stomach churned.

To my surprise, the recovering men and women I met were tolerant and accepting of my rabid atheism. At their suggestion, I took actions which, seemingly, had nothing to do with God. I made what for me was remarkable progress.

Coming to believe in a Power greater than myself was a slow and arduous process. It took several years to let go of my old ideas and open my mind to new ones. When I finally did come to believe, not just with my mind but with all my heart, that's when my life began anew.

THOUGHT FOR TODAY: I am grateful that today my beliefs are my own.

When we reached the threshold of belief in a Higher Power, the one suggestion, more than any other, that encouraged us to step forward was that we choose a God of *our own understanding*. We were relieved that we didn't have to conform to other people's beliefs—that there were no boundaries or restrictions to hold us back. If there had been, many of us would have been hard-pressed to make a start.

Given this personal freedom and flexibility, it became possible to develop a faith that worked. Some of us sought to reaffirm or begin a new relationship with the God of our religious upbringing. Those who had never formed an understanding of God, or who were unsure, searched and listened open-mindedly for ideas.

In my own case, it was suggested that I try to visualize the recovery group as a Higher Power. If I wasn't comfortable with that concept, I could choose the ocean, the sun and moon, symmetry and balance in the universe, the life force, or all that is good in the world. It didn't matter what I chose to believe in initially, I was told, as long as it was something greater than myself.

THOUGHT FOR TODAY: As I continue to grow and change, so does my understanding of God.

Coming to Believe

February 16

Now that we have welcomed God into our lives, all that was previously impossible has become possible. With each passing day, we believe more deeply in His power to bring about positive and long-lasting changes.

We have found release from the chronic fear and self-loathing that kept us imprisoned for so long. We have been offered freedom and a new happiness, and have come to know the true meaning of inner peace.

Today, because we are in touch with God within us, it is far easier to follow our intuition and make the right choices. Whenever we are confused or uncertain, we know we can rely on Him for guidance.

Thanks to God, our lives today have meaning and purpose. Self-pity and despair have given way to a sense of usefulness. We have grown less self-centered and more giving. Learning to care about ourselves has enabled us to care about others.

Since discovering the rewards of faith, we experience every dimension of our lives in wholly different and more fulfilling ways than when we relied exclusively on our own resources.

THOUGHT FOR TODAY: My mind and heart remain open to God.

I could tell that these recovering people had "been there." So when they assured me that wellness was possible through reliance on God and the application of spiritual principles, I was somewhat hopeful. But later on, when they elaborated in more personal terms, hope faded into confusion and even discouragement. The problem, for those of us with dysfunctional backgrounds, was that our heads were filled with negative preconceptions.

Even if there had been a professed belief in God at home, there never had been any real communication, commitment, or constancy on the part of our parents. When they did speak of God, it was usually in anger: "If there is a God, He sure isn't looking out for this family!"

Besides that, self-reliance had been our code for years. Many of us also felt unworthy of God's attention. We couldn't imagine turning to Him in the ways our friends had described.

What we had to do was wipe the slate clean, so to speak, in order to give ourselves and God a chance. We had to consciously put aside all of our misconceptions so that we could become receptive to new ideas. We had to continue listening open-mindedly, until hope returned and eventually became truth.

THOUGHT FOR TODAY: Nothing hinders my progress more than closed-mindedness.

Coming to Believe

February 18

Affirmation

I can't see you or touch you, God, but there's no question in my mind and heart that you are with me now and forever. There were times when I doubted your love, even your existence, but today you are the most tangible reality in my life.

I came to you, reluctantly at first, as a fearful and despairing soul. Although I had but a small degree of open-mindedness, you heard me as clearly then as you do now. Over time, through your loving kindness, I have been transformed into a productive participant in life, someone who can make a difference.

For years and years I tried desperately and fruitlessly to bring about change in and around me. Now that I accept my personal limitations, life has ceased to be an endless struggle. So much more is possible since I have become willing to rely on you for guidance, courage, and strength.

I pray, dear God, that my faith will remain true and strong. I pray that I may continue to grow spiritually, one step at a time and one day at a time.

THOUGHT FOR TODAY: When I compare my life today with the way it once was, I am filled with gratitude for God's loving Presence.

8

Attitude

To all upon my way, Day after day,
Let me be joy, be hope. Let my life sing!

—MARY CAROLYN DAVIES

February 19

For more years than I care to remember, I lived and breathed negativity. I felt contempt and hostility for everything and everyone; I had faith in nothing and no one. Needless to say, my outlook on life kept me miserable.

Sometimes I think back and feel sad for the person I was, and for the years I wasted. But I know that for some reason my life was meant to be that way. Recovery and faith had to come to me gradually, and in God's time.

Indeed, it was my emerging faith and subsequent actions that ultimately made it possible for my attitudes to undergo a radical transformation.

I don't pretend for a moment to have a constantly sunlit spirit, or that each day dawns like an inspirational hymn. Like most people, I find myself slipping back into old ways of thinking from time to time.

Thankfully, however, for the most part my attitude is optimistic rather than pessimistic, and high-spirited rather than mean-spirited. It is this momentous change, perhaps more than any other, that makes my life so enjoyable today.

THOUGHT FOR TODAY: Changed attitudes can mean a changed life.

Attitude

No matter how many times we've been through it before, we always seem to forget that a bad attitude has the potential for ruining just about any kind of experience.

The negative attitude we bring into a business meeting, for example, keeps us from listening and participating. Instead, we end up sullenly judging everyone. In the same way, our gloomy outlook at a family get-together causes concern and even spoils everyone else's good time.

Is there something we can do to turn the tide when we are being swept away by a negative attitude? The first thing we can do is to stop and think seriously for a moment about where our attitude is taking us. Chances are, we'll decide we really don't want to go there.

We can next ask ourselves if there is anything we can do to change the way we feel. What can we do to improve the meeting? How can we stop thinking about ourselves, and get involved in positive ways with our family members? Finally, we can try to sort out the little annoyances that have shaped our negative attitudes, and thereby diminish their importance and influence.

THOUGHT FOR TODAY: It is rarely possible to alter another person, a place, or a thing. It is always possible to alter an attitude.

Attitude

February 21

Living in the now—it's quite a contrast to the way we used to live. What a pleasure to be present and accounted for, mentally as well as physically. What a difference in the quality of our lives when we can give our complete concentration and energy to what we are doing, and fully experience each moment.

For a long time, our unhealthy attitudes about the past prevented us from living successfully in the present. We were preoccupied with memories of earlier years—with what had occurred and how we had been adversely affected. We indulged in self-pity and even martyrdom.

Perhaps our most damaging attitude was the one that told us we were entitled to feel sorry for ourselves. Only when we realized that we were being cheated out of a life did we attempt to change that negative outlook. At that point, we began to move from the past into the present.

Today we see our life history as a stepping-stone rather than a stumbling block. The past is an irrevocable part of us, true enough. We still have a choice, however, as to how much or how little importance we give it in the present.

THOUGHT FOR TODAY: Is my attitude toward the past tarnishing the present?

Our attitudes usually are developed within ourselves. They are formed by our thoughts and feelings,
our foibles and fancies. But they can also be greatly
influenced by other people.

We all know from experience how easy it is to be
pulled down by a partner's cynical outlook, or to be
drawn into the negativity of a friend. In the work-
place, especially, we're all familiar with the kind of
peer pressure that encourages us to bad-mouth the
job and spread discontent.

When we're caught in the middle like that, it can
be difficult to hold on to our values and principles.
Sometimes it seems so much more convenient to just
"go along."

However, when we compromise our integrity in
that way, we forsake our true selves with a highly
damaging form of dishonesty. And we end up just as
miserable as those around us.

If that happens, we may be tempted to blame
others for "making us" feel cynical and negative. But
no one can force a bad attitude on anyone else. Each
of us is our own person. How we view the world, and
how we react to the emotional pressures surrounding
us, is our responsibility.

THOUGHT FOR TODAY: Adopting someone else's
bad attitude is people-pleasing at its worst.

February 23

The troubles I have from time to time are more often the result of my attitudes and reaction to events than the events themselves. I've learned that the hard way. I'm also beginning to discover where my attitudes come from, and that makes it easier to change them.

Not too long ago, for example, I realized the extent to which my character defects influence and even wholly create attitudes that can rule my life and ruin my days. When I am angry, fearful, or envious—when I am closed-minded and filled with pride—my attitudes are bound to reflect those traits. So one of the best ways to overcome such negative attitudes, I've found, is to work on my character defects.

I've also learned that my attitudes are frequently shaped by my perception of reality. The better able I am to see and accept things as they truly are, the less I'm troubled by distorted and damaging attitudes.

The bottom line is that I have far more control over my attitudes than I ever thought possible. Once I understand the origin and anatomy of an attitude, I can do something about it.

THOUGHT FOR TODAY: I will try to be more aware of my attitudes and their causes.

We used to get up each morning filled with dread rather than anticipation. Even before we were fully awake, our minds had begun to churn with gloomy thoughts and nameless fears. By the time our feet hit the floor, our attitude had been shaped and set.

In truth, we still have those kinds of mornings occasionally. But they have become the exception rather than the rule. For the most part, we now face each day positively and optimistically.

It's not that we wake up with a smile on our lips and ebullience in our hearts. Before we actually face the day, we take the time to develop the kind of attitude that will allow us to get the most out of it. Here are some of the things we find helpful.

We say a prayer, asking God to direct our thoughts and actions, and to keep us on course.

If we can't help thinking ahead, we try to do so realistically. We focus on positive events that await us, rather than on negative potentials.

We acknowledge that it's largely up to us whether we have a good day or a bad day.

THOUGHT FOR TODAY: I will take the time, right now, to shape a positive attitude.

Affirmation

Today I choose to be enthusiastic and faithful, for I know full well that my attitude will shape my day. If I remain in this positive frame of mind, each experience I have is sure to be that much more enjoyable, and the challenges I face will be that much less formidable.

If something unforeseen dampens my spirits, I'll remember that my attitude is still a matter of choice. I will try to be realistic, searching for the positive rather than dwelling on the negative. I will get involved with other people and share my feelings. I will say a prayer.

By keeping God in my thoughts, I'm much more likely to maintain an affirmative outlook. It's been proven to me again and again that He has a plan for my highest good, so I can't help but be uplifted and faith-filled when I turn to Him.

Wherever I go and whatever I do today, I will try to be generous with my positive energy. In so doing, I will bring out the best in myself and, hopefully, the best in others as well.

THOUGHT FOR TODAY: In all my relationships and activities, my attitude will make a difference.

9

Self-image

The precept, "Know yourself," was not solely in-tended to obviate the pride of mankind; but likewise that we might understand our own worth.

—CICERO

February 26

For years I wasn't happy with what I "saw" in myself. I didn't recognize that the problem stemmed from a poor self-image, etched long before. I didn't realize that the way I perceived myself could be changed for the better.

Only in recovery did I begin to understand that a negative self-image is very rarely an accurate reflection of reality. On the contrary, it is simply a belief system we likely developed about ourselves when we were young.

If we were fortunate enough to receive encouragement, support, and love on a consistent basis, chances are we grew up with a positive self-image. If on the other hand we were constantly belittled, humiliated, and undermined, just the opposite was true.

That is what happened to me as a child, and my poor self-image stayed with me well into adulthood. I reached a major turning point when I learned that my problem was not the way my parents treated me "back then," but how I "see" myself today. Just as I developed a belief system about myself based on what was available to me as a child, so I can now build a new belief system based on today's reality.

THOUGHT FOR TODAY: Is my self-image an accurate reflection of the real me and my life today?

Why is it so important to work toward developing and maintaining a positive self-image? If we think about it for a moment, the answer is clear: The way we perceive ourselves greatly influences the way we treat ourselves, as well as the way we relate to other people.

How does a poor self-image affect our lives day by day? For one thing, we are constantly driven to prove ourselves. We seek perfection, which we never achieve, and therefore we're always on the defensive. Of course, this makes us highly vulnerable to stress. It's as if we're forever behind the eight ball.

A poor self-image also causes us to alienate ourselves. Since we don't want others to "see what we see," we hide behind all sorts of behavioral disguises. Moreover, it's all but impossible for us to accept compliments or take credit for things we've done well.

Because we're such experts at judging ourselves harshly—no matter what we do, it's not good enough—we tend to judge others just as unfairly. This doesn't do a whole lot for our relationships. Worst of all, because our poor self-image tells us we're not deserving, we deny ourselves the opportunity to be comfortable and happy in the world.

THOUGHT FOR TODAY: No matter what I do or who I am with today, I'm not going to judge myself.

Self-image

Failed relationships, job difficulties, financial crises, emotional upheavals. These traumas, along with deeply grooved messages from childhood, contributed to the tarnished self-images we brought with us into recovery.

But now we're making progress and our lives have changed dramatically. We're learning to practice self-restraint and patience. We're becoming less selfish and more giving. We're taking responsibility. And our self-image is changing along with everything else. Where we once saw ourselves as sick, suffering, second-class citizens, we now see ourselves as healthy, capable, and deserving.

Unfortunately, a few people in our lives—family members in particular—are unable to recognize the positive changes. They still see us as we once were. In our frustration, we may be tempted to end relationships abruptly, or to fall back into familiar roles ("bad boy," "sick girl") to avoid confrontation.

This can be a critical time for us. In order to continue our progress and build healthier relationships, it's important that we remain true to our new way of life. It may be necessary to open new lines of communication, assertively detailing the changes we're making. If we can do this with understanding and the proper motives, it's likely that support will be forthcoming.

THOUGHT FOR TODAY: If someone I'm close to still sees me and treats me as if I haven't made substantial progress, I will stand up for myself.

I saw a friend at a party and when we greeted each other I told her how terrific she looked. "Thanks," she said with a smile, patting herself on the hip. "I went out and bought myself a whole new wardrobe and I feel really great about it."

She reminded me of how heavy she had been several years earlier because of compulsive overeating. "When I finally got into recovery and became abstinent, it wasn't all that difficult to drop fifty pounds and maintain an ideal weight," she said. "It's been a lot harder to change my self-image."

Until recently, my friend explained, she had still perceived herself as overweight, even though she was not. She continued to buy clothes in extra-large sizes, felt that she was taking up too much room in cars and elevators and, overall, remained painfully self-conscious.

"But that was just the tip of the iceberg," she said. "My self-image was lagging way behind the physical, emotional, and spiritual changes taking place in my life. I still saw myself as sick and unworthy, and I treated myself accordingly. You know, baggy clothes—that sort of thing.

"I've really been working on this," she added, "and being willing to spend money on clothes that really fit—that's a sign of major progress."

THOUGHT FOR TODAY: To keep an up-to-date self-image, it's important to take stock and gauge my progress from time to time.

March 2

Taking comfort in the familiar—even when it's harmful and degrading—is something we all do on occasion. That's probably why so many of us cling tenaciously to poor self-images long after we've begun to turn our lives around.

Let's face it: Sticking with the status quo certainly can seem safer and easier. After all, we know the rules of the game; we don't have to take risks, so there's no chance we'll "fail." We don't have to upset relationships with people who like things just as they are. We don't have to become vulnerable and risk rejection or disapproval. We don't have to give up the familiar roles—"black sheep," "bumbler," "victim"—that helped us fit in and get by for so long. In short, we don't have to find new ways of relating to ourselves and others.

The point is, while it may *seem* safer and easier to stick with our old self-perceptions, just the opposite is true. A poor self-image, if left untreated, gets progressively worse. Over time, it becomes an ever-larger obstacle to our progress. It feeds on negativity, absorbing only self-deprecating thoughts while deflecting positive ones.

THOUGHT FOR TODAY: It takes more than simple resolve to change outdated perceptions of ourselves. It takes courage, hard work, discipline—and willingness.

Self-image   70

Although it may appear that there is an enormous chasm between the way we perceive ourselves and the way we actually are, there is much we can do to successfully bridge the gap.

One of the most effective tools is a written inventory, by which we fearlessly and thoroughly examine our assets and liabilities. We may be tempted to use this tool as a whipping post, by exaggerating our defects and ignoring our strengths. So we need to take special care to look at ourselves honestly, and not place value judgments on what we find.

An inventory allows us to see ourselves realistically—perhaps for the first time—and to determine where we actually stand in the world. Consequently, when out-of-date negative images of ourselves surface from time to time, we're less likely to take them seriously.

We also can work toward bridging the gap on a daily basis—by accepting compliments graciously, by taking credit when it is deserved, and by acknowledging our achievements and progress. We can try to see ourselves through the eyes of friends, neighbors, and loved ones, who readily see and admire qualities in us that we may tend to overlook.

THOUGHT FOR TODAY: An honest inventory of personal assets and liabilities will lead me toward an improved self-image.

Self-image

March 4

Affirmation

Day by day I am developing a new belief system about myself based on present reality. I take conscious note of my accomplishments and good works in order to further my progress with encouragement, support, and loving kindness.

I will remember that my self-image greatly influences how I treat myself and how I function in the world. As I approach unfolding challenges and opportunities, I will see myself as the strong, capable, and worthy person that I really am.

I will remain aware of my many positive qualities, putting aside thoughts and pressures that have the potential to undermine me and slow my growth. I will recognize those self-defeating messages for what they are, without becoming emotionally involved. I will focus on truth—on the healthy and productive person I am becoming.

I affirm the importance of my spiritual being, which has become an integral part of my self-image. Throughout this day I will remember that no matter how I perceive myself, to God I am ever deserving, ever special, and ever loved.

THOUGHT FOR TODAY: As I focus on changing my self-image, I will not lose sight of unchanging spiritual truths.

10

Breaking the Chain

The past is but the beginning of a beginning, and all that is and has been is but the twilight of the dawn.

—HERBERT GEORGE WELLS

March 5

At various stages of my recovery I was blessed with insights which led to new awarenesses, greater willingness to make changes, and accelerated progress. One such insight allowed me to better understand my upbringing and free myself of long-standing misconceptions, guilt, and resentments.

I finally realized at a gut level that my parents treated me as they did largely because of the circumstances and influences of their own upbringings. They didn't offer love because they had not received love themselves. They were abusive because they had been abused. For the first time, it became clear to me that the pattern extended back over generations.

Needless to say, that insight didn't automatically improve my relationship with my parents, nor did it heal long-festering emotional wounds overnight.

What I did experience almost immediately, however, were deep feelings of gratitude. For I had been given the opportunity in recovery to step back, to see my family history in perspective, to deal constructively with destructive behavioral patterns, and to break the chain once and for all. I am grateful that I have been given the opportunity to pass on health rather than sickness.

THOUGHT FOR TODAY: The ripple effect of my recovery sends forth spiritual and emotional wellness.

Over and over we vowed that we would never be like our parents. We would never be violent and hurtful. We would never be cold or inattentive. We would never *ever* drink or use drugs the way they did.

Time passed. We crossed a line and, in spite of our good intentions, we eventually became abusive, neglectful, and uncaring toward our own loved ones. Some of us developed serious problems with alcohol and drugs. Although our youthful vows had been sincere, they remained unfulfilled or were broken. We ended up just like our parents.

In retrospect, we never had a chance as youngsters to choose a different path. We learned by example, unconsciously following in the footsteps of our primary role models. We also had ambivalent and confused feelings about the things that went on in our homes. While we abhorred the drunken violence that we saw, for example, we thought it was perfectly normal to drink in the morning.

In recovery we have new role models. We're gradually giving up our confusion and old ideas about how to live and relate to others. We're experiencing an entirely new way of life.

THOUGHT FOR TODAY: It's not necessary—or even advantageous—for me to make long-term vows in recovery. All I need is the willingness to change, one day at a time.

March 7

For more years than we care to remember, the turmoil in our families has caused us great distress. We've wanted so badly to break the chain of misery and restore the family to health. We've sometimes wished it was in our power to bring about change in others.

But of course we don't have that kind of power. As much as we'd like to, we can't change our family members or make them happy. We can't make up for what our parents didn't get. We can't enlighten them; we can't rescue them from self-destructive behavior. We can't fix them, period.

What we can do, with God's help, is change ourselves. We can find a new direction and a new support system. We can find peace and a limitless source of spiritual strength.

We seek these changes not for our family's sake, but for our own sake. By discovering our true selves and building inner security as part of our spiritual recovery, it becomes possible for us to transmit health and harmony rather than to perpetuate rancor and discord.

THOUGHT FOR TODAY: The example of my recovery can make a difference in the lives of those around me.

Breaking the Chain

Because we grew up surrounded by dysfunction, the odds were strong that we would become dysfunctional ourselves. And we did. Prior to recovery, we had already begun to forge new links in the chain that bound us so tightly to our family sickness.

Though unaware of it, some of us choose partners just like the parents we resented so bitterly. Perhaps our hidden motive was to finally win the love and approval that had always been withheld. Or perhaps it was simply a case of attracting and being attracted to someone as emotionally "messed up" as we were.

As adults, some of us unconsciously re-created the same sort of crisis-laden situations we experienced as children. The characters and staging were different, but the behavior and aftermath were the same. We treated our spouses or partners just as our mothers and fathers treated each other. The upheavals and even the illnesses in our lives paralleled those in their lives. We ended up with the same insecurities—external as well as internal—that plagued our parents.

Thank God, we were finally able to see what was happening. Thank God, we were offered another choice.

THOUGHT FOR TODAY: I am destined to be an individual in my own right, and to follow my own path.

March 9

We've chosen a new path and are making major changes. Some of them have distanced us from our parents. Does this mean they don't belong in our lives anymore?

Not at all. We *want* the relationship with our parents to continue, albeit with new ground rules. We are family, after all, and more than likely we still care about each other. In addition, we can experience rewarding personal growth as the result of our efforts to redirect or reestablish these important relationships. In fact, when we apply new solutions to old problems on the family proving ground, we can benefit in very specific ways.

We can benefit greatly

. . . if we're able to be patient and understanding when our parents react with confusion or anger to our new direction.

. . . if we communicate our feelings honestly, forthrightly, yet sensitively when our parents make unreasonable demands of us.

. . . if we stand up for ourselves and hold our ground when our parents try to seduce us into assuming old roles.

Working on the relationship with our parents in these ways takes courage and persistence, to be sure, but our efforts can signal the beginning of a closer, freer, and healthier bond for all concerned.

THOUGHT FOR TODAY: I will do my part to improve and maintain my relationship with my parent(s).

Hard as it may be to accept, there are times when we no longer can afford to be actively involved with our parents. The price is much too high.

We've done everything in our power to help them understand and accept our new way of life. But they remain completely disapproving and inflexible. Some are so locked into their old ways of relating to us that they are severely threatened and even outraged by our transformation. Some see the changes as a personal attack; they defend themselves by responding with vicious insults, accusations, and exaggerations.

When we're in an untenable situation such as this, all the progress we've made is in jeopardy. The pain alone is almost beyond endurance at times, and we may be tempted to regress. Clearly, we can't put off what we've been dreading.

In some extreme cases, where contact of any kind results in disaster, we may have to end all involvement. Usually, however, a reduction in contact will suffice.

Saying good-bye to a destructive relationship—especially one involving a parent—can be one of the most difficult and heartbreaking challenges we face in our new life. But it can also be liberating and reassuring to know that we have the willingness and courage to do whatever it takes to further our recovery.

THOUGHT FOR TODAY: I pray for wisdom and courage to make the right choices concerning my relationships.

March 11

Affirmation

God has made it possible for me to become my own person. I trust my instincts and capabilities, and have been given courage to follow the course that is right for me. The chain has been broken. I now am free to develop new values, new goals, and a whole new purpose in life.

I have decided without reservation that I want something different for myself. I choose not to participate in and perpetuate unhealthy family roles and rituals. I realize that it is necessary to learn new principles, to find new role models, to establish a new support system—to actively participate in my own recovery.

God continues to bless me with new insights and opportunities. Now that I see my family history in true perspective, I am able to be more understanding and tolerant. Now that I realize the extent of my powerlessness over others, I am able to focus on inner change. Now that I am getting well myself, I am able to pass along health rather than sickness.

THOUGHT FOR TODAY: I will celebrate my new freedom; I will celebrate my new purpose; I will celebrate the new me.

11

Happiness

The mere sense of living is joy enough.
—EMILY DICKINSON

March 12

Several weeks after I got sober, I listened intently as a man described his recovery from addiction. When he told a joke at his own expense, the audience erupted with laughter. I laughed harder and longer than anyone.

It was the first time in ages that I had laughed like that. I recall it as a wonderfully freeing experience, one that seemed to shake loose and release much of the pain that had been bottled up inside me. At that moment I was supremely happy.

That experience, as unremarkable as it may have been, led to one of my first awarenesses in sobriety. Life had always been deadly serious to me. I had been so immersed in myself and my problems that I couldn't see or feel anything beyond my own little world of pain. The reason I hadn't laughed for so long was that I hadn't allowed myself to do so.

If I was going to have more and more moments of happiness in recovery, I realized, I would have to give up the illusion of control and let down my guard. I would have to stop taking myself so seriously.

THOUGHT FOR TODAY: I will free my spirit with laughter. I will allow myself to be happy.

We're all familiar with coin-operated telescopes—the kind that can be found at tourist attractions. We also know the disappointment that comes when the timer clicks off, the eyepiece goes black, and we discover we've been looking in the wrong direction.

Many of us have had similarly disappointing experiences in our search for happiness—and for the same reason. We were focusing on the wrong things. We equated happiness with achievement and accumulation, so we went after it by seeking the "right" partner, job, or bank balance. We would be happy, we thought, when we had success and status.

It's not that we hadn't been exposed to the fundamental truth that happiness must come from within ourselves, rather than from outside sources. It seems, however, that each of us had to become convinced of this reality in our own way, and in our own time.

Perhaps we actually had to buy that special car, win that special partner, and move into that special house. Perhaps it was necessary to become disillusioned one more time before we became willing to "put in another quarter," pivot the telescope one hundred eighty degrees, and approach happiness with an entirely different point of view.

THOUGHT FOR TODAY: Have I shifted focus and begun to look within for happiness?

Happiness

March 14

More often than we'd care to admit, our spirits would sink as we wondered if we'd ever be happy. We dreamed of being happily married, of being happy in our jobs, of being happy people. We thought of happiness in absolute terms—either you have it or you don't.

Because we demanded *"total happiness"* or *"happiness forever,"* we frequently missed out on happiness altogether. We wanted nothing less than the entire treasure chest; as a result we allowed countless individual jewels to slip through our fingers.

As we've matured, we've come to understand that genuine happiness is not an always feeling, but a sometimes feeling.

We've given up trying to be happy all of the time. Instead, we now savor and are grateful for the sights, sounds, and experiences that can bring us moments of happiness each day. A flowering tree, a starry night, a warm greeting, heading home . . .

What is more, we no longer attempt to plan and program happiness as if it is something that can be forced into a daily agenda. And now that we've set aside our unrealistic expectations, we're better able to enjoy happiness whenever and wherever it comes our way.

THOUGHT FOR TODAY: I will experience this day, moment by moment, with joyful acceptance.

Some of us approached the necessity of a spiritual recovery with considerable apprehension. The actions we were urged to take—prayer and meditation, personal inventory, and making amends, to name several—seemed to reflect a life that was bound to be restrictive and tedious.

As it turned out, just the opposite was true. Granted, it takes discipline, hard work, and courage to "clean house" and learn to trust God. But now that we have successfully achieved these goals, we are being rewarded with excitement and happiness beyond anything we have ever known.

The very actions we feared taking have widened rather than narrowed our horizons. They have unburdened us of the secrets, guilt, and resentments that weighed so heavily upon us for so long.

Our life today is by no means boring and restrictive. On the contrary, we've become keenly aware that the world around us—and we ourselves—are perpetually changing, growing, and unfolding. There is always something new to discover and appreciate.

Today we say *yes* to the spiritual way of life, convinced that it is meant to be exhilarating and fulfilling.

THOUGHT FOR TODAY: I will reflect on the excitement and joy that my spiritual journey is bringing to my life.

March 16

"I know I'm romanticizing this," a friend was saying, "but when I look back at my childhood, I see myself as a caged bird. A bird that never had the chance to know the joy of free flight.

"I had no idea what it meant to be happy when I was a child," he continued. "I knew what it felt like to be serious, or sad, and I knew a lot about guilt. That goes without saying.

"Then, without any warning, childhood was over. When I got out on my own, I had to actually learn from scratch how to be happy. I had to learn how to fly. It was a trial-and-error sort of thing, finding out what gave me pleasure, and what didn't.

"To give you an example, for a while I thought I could be happy being by myself, doing things on my own. Then I found that I was much happier around other people, doing things together—like going to a movie, hiking, even helping someone move.

"But the biggest lesson I learned," he said, "is that my happiness doesn't *depend* on other people—it doesn't depend on the actions or judgments of anyone else. Whether or not I'm happy today is entirely up to me."

THOUGHT FOR TODAY: I will give thought to what makes me happy and, if necessary, I will redirect my energies toward achieving it.

When I flash back to milestones in my past, the memories are more often painful than pleasant. There were good times, to be sure, but I mostly remember anticlimaxes and disappointments—celebrations gone wrong.

One way or another, I almost always managed to turn happiness into unhappiness, and success into failure. This pattern dogged my heels for many years. As I understand it today, low self-esteem and lingering guilt made me feel that I wasn't entitled to carefree vacations, joyful celebrations, or career-related accolades.

Feelings of happiness were always linked with another emotion: *fear.* I feared that my happiness would be quickly taken from me, or that something disastrous would occur to counteract it. In other words, happiness caused me anxiety. That's why I often unwittingly sabotaged it.

Thankfully, yesterday's memories are quite different from today's realities. For the most part, I can truly enjoy special occasions and the pleasure they bring. Nevertheless, it is still necessary for me to periodically reaffirm that I am deserving of happiness, and that I still have the power of choice—to accept it, or send it away.

THOUGHT FOR TODAY: Does happiness or the prospect of it still make me uncomfortable?

March 18

Affirmation

I affirm that I am entitled to happiness. There is nothing about me—either inherently or by virtue of past misdeeds—that makes me undeserving. I invite and welcome happiness into my life today.

In the past I tended to take myself extremely seriously, seeing everything as either black or white. These days I try to be easygoing, and sensitive to the humor and ironies that color the world around me.

The source of true and lasting happiness is within myself. I will go directly to that place today. If I become unhappy, I will try to uncover the causes of my discontent. Chances are, I'll find them within as well. If I become unhappy, it will probably be because I'm not getting my own way, because I've chosen a negative attitude, or because my expectations have run amok.

My happiness is no longer contingent on the actions or attitudes of others. Today I am responsible for my own happiness. It's up to me to discover and build upon the states of mind and activities that bring wonder and joy into my life.

THOUGHT FOR TODAY: I am deserving of happiness, as are all of God's children.

12

Denial

Illusions commend themselves to us because they save us pain and allow us to enjoy pleasure instead. We must therefore accept it without complaint when they sometimes collide with a bit of reality against which they are dashed to pieces.

—SIGMUND FREUD

March 19

Most of us are familiar with the obvious ways in which denial of reality blocks our progress. But our illusions can take over and cause harm in subtle ways as well, especially regarding past and present family relationships.

To this day, some of us have difficulty admitting that our families were dysfunctional, that our parents were abusive, and that we were damaged emotionally. We may still rationalize that we were treated coldly or disdainfully because our parents didn't want to spoil us, or were too busy. We may go so far as to distort the reality of physical beatings into a belief that "it was for our own good."

Why do some of us still avoid the truth about our upbringing? Perhaps we don't want to experience the initial pain of facing reality. Perhaps we're afraid of changes that may occur in existing family relationships, unpleasant and harmful as they may be. Or perhaps we don't want to feel guilty; after all, our parents did give us life, did raise us, and may still even subsidize us.

The fact remains, however, that denial can be a formidable barrier on the road to recovery. We may be off to a good start, but we will assuredly lose ground if we remain unwilling or unable to face reality.

THOUGHT FOR TODAY: We slip into denial to protect ourselves from painful truths. But denial ultimately causes us even greater pain.

Denial   **90**

The denial network in my family was intricate, far-reaching, and effective. It was as if we had taken blood oaths and sworn each other to secrecy and silence. Our purpose was to present the best possible face not only to the outside world, but to ourselves as well.

I learned early that denial is an acceptable and even desirable method of dealing with unpleasant truths and painful realities. As a child, I was expected to go along with the rest of my family in overlooking my parents' contempt for each other, in ignoring their abusive behavior, and in pretending that everything was just fine.

By growing up under these circumstances, I learned not only to deny certain truths about my family, but also about myself. I learned to be dishonest, to repress my feelings, and to disregard my character flaws. I moved further and further away from reality as I carried these practices into adulthood.

To break a lifelong pattern of denial, I was told, I must be willing to share my secrets and admit my faults to myself and others; only then can the wall of isolation and denial finally crumble.

THOUGHT FOR TODAY: I will break my lifelong pattern of secrecy and silence. I will "blow the whistle" on denial.

March 21

Thankfully, the move out of denial into self-awareness and acceptance doesn't come all at once. The recovery process is most often a series of awakenings—some welcome and exciting, others painful and difficult to face.

Certain truths about ourselves can be the hardest to swallow. We learn about character defects and begin to identify them in ourselves, for example, but we may stop short at acknowledging the extent to which those flaws adversely affect our lives.

We readily admit that we are short-tempered, but refuse to make the connection between our frequent angry outbursts and the sense of disquiet and inner turmoil we so often feel.

We come to realize that we're people-pleasers, yet won't admit that our behavior in that regard causes discomfort and a loss of self-respect.

We know that we tend to be intolerant, but deny that this character flaw is responsible for the lack of harmony in our relationships.

There is no need to be discouraged as these truths become gradually evident. So long as we remain willing to confront and work through our various levels of denial as they surface, we are bound to move forward.

THOUGHT FOR TODAY: When conflicts occur or emotional difficulties arise, I will try to determine if my character defects are involved.

Denial   92

Denial was our "deep cover" from reality. We developed an entire life-style and image to justify our false beliefs. We did everything we could to make the facts fit the illusions.

The problem was that we actually fooled no one. We couldn't help revealing and exposing ourselves with out-of-control actions or addictions. On top of that, people kept interfering with our plan by trying to remind us of who we *really* were.

We realize now that they simply wanted to help us. At the time, however, it seemed they were the enemy. The closer they brought the light of truth, the more threatened we were—and the deeper we burrowed into our denial.

What a relief to finally come in from the cold! What a relief to learn that there's far more to life than just staying alive.

These days, instead of trying to defend illusions and behavior that cause us problems, we take steps to become rid of them. We're willing and able to be our true selves and to see things as they really are.

THOUGHT FOR TODAY: Denial seemed necessary to survival, but it was almost the death of us.

March 23

As practicing alcoholics and addicts we used every conceivable excuse and rationalization to deny our dependencies. Drinking, using drugs, gambling, compulsive overeating—whatever the substance or behavior—it had become the most important part of our lives.

From today's vantage point of health and sanity, those former expressions of our denial seem transparent and pathetic. At the time, however, we had little choice. Denial, as the primary symptom of our illness, had taken over mind and body.

Although we knew deep down that something was terribly wrong, we stayed in denial because we feared the consequences of recovery. We clung desperately to our addictions because we couldn't imagine life without them.

When we finally hit bottom and surrendered, the first and hardest step into a new life was admitting without reservation that we were in fact addicted and ill. We see now that without that essential concession, recovery would have been impossible.

Today life is richer and more joyous than we ever dreamed possible. As amazing as it sometimes seems, our attitudes and actions have shifted one hundred eighty degrees. Just as we went to any length in the past to deny our addictions, so we now go to any length to progress in recovery.

THOUGHT FOR TODAY: I can guard against the return of denial by remembering where I came from, and by being grateful for where I am now.

I once worked in a skid row liquor store. When I opened up at six every morning, the same group of men were lined up outside. As they shuffled in to exchange nickels and dimes for pints of wine, I felt sad for the life they had to lead. I knew I drank a lot, but it never entered my mind that I was well on my way to joining them.

It wasn't until I got sober years later that I began to understand that *denial* was not just a word in the dictionary, but an elaborate system of rationalizations and illusions. Because of denial, my alcoholism also progressed to early morning line-ups for cheap wine.

In recovery, I eventually saw that I had been in denial about more than my addiction. I had also refused to face the emotional damage I had suffered. And I had become a master at hiding from my character defects and problems.

My denial didn't suddenly disappear. It was necessary for me to listen to people with similar problems and experiences. By doing this, it became possible to identify, admit, and begin to work on my own flaws and fears. I was then able to gradually move into reality.

THOUGHT FOR TODAY: I will look to others for help in moving out of denial and into the real world.

Denial

Affirmation

Each new truth that I welcome is another stepping-stone toward self-discovery. Where once I layered my life with denial to avoid pain and challenge, I now face each day's reality with a clear view and a trusting heart.

Today I celebrate reality. It is there that I can find additional pieces in the mosaic of my life, and thus gain greater understanding of the person I am becoming. Each time I discover a piece that fits, I come closer to envisioning the beauty and perfection of God's design.

As I interact with others at home, on the job, or in social situations, I will not allow myself to be swept along by undercurrents of tacit denial. I will hold fast to the solid foundation of truth and honesty in my new life.

No matter where I go or what I do, nothing will tempt me to alter my consciousness of reality, or to distort my perspective. It is my intention to be present and aware, in order to fully discover and appreciate the world within and around me.

THOUGHT FOR TODAY: Denial is no longer a refuge or even an option. I will find comfort and strength in reality.

13

Anger

Give not reins to your inflamed passions; take time and a little delay; impetuosity manages all things badly.

—Publius Statius

March 26

When I experience moments or hours of contentment and serenity, I rarely take them for granted. The contrast between those peaceful times and my years of rage remains far too vivid for that.

While I don't dwell morbidly on my explosive behavior—the ways I railed at the world and everyone in it—I never want to forget how I suffered because of my anger. It's unlikely that I will, because I still carry emotional and physical scars to remind me.

As time has passed, I've learned a great deal about the anger that ruled me from childhood into recovery. I have learned first that the anger I felt toward people, places, and things was, in reality, anger at myself. That anger was born of self-loathing and insecurity.

Most importantly, I've come to realize that my anger is usually a cover-up for other emotions such as fear, hurt, and confusion. When I start getting angry these days, I try to pause and ask myself, "What's really going on? What am I afraid of?" Most of the time this not only defuses my anger, but helps me confront and deal with my underlying feelings.

THOUGHT FOR TODAY: I am grateful that my peaceful moments far outweigh my angry ones.

Anger   98

For a long time we felt we were doing the right thing by repressing or denying our anger. Perhaps we weren't even aware of our anger! It had been drummed into us, growing up, that it was an emotion better kept to oneself. When it overflowed, we were punished.

As adults, some of us held on to the belief that anger is an unattractive and unacceptable emotion; we stayed convinced that if we expressed it, people would punish us with disapproval.

Of course, we paid a big price on the days we repressed our anger. It built within us until we eventually blew up. We lashed out at people not even remotely involved. Our internalized anger made us emotionally and physically ill—it caused headaches, insomnia, ulcers. Repressed anger tainted just about everything—our relationships, our performance, our ability to enjoy and appreciate the good things.

We have learned to avoid such problems by acknowledging and dealing with our anger in constructive ways. We don't let it get out of hand, but we do look at it honestly and forthrightly. We don't indulge in explosive outbursts, but we do express our anger appropriately when it serves a purpose.

THOUGHT FOR TODAY: Anger becomes a problem only when I deny it, repress it, or let it get out of control.

March 28

A new friend called me one morning to apologize for losing her temper at me the night before. I had accidentally backed my car into her car. Although there was no damage, it really set her off.

"I hardly ever act like that anymore," she said toward the end of the conversation. "But you should have seen me a few years ago. They called me 'The Angry Redhead.'"

She told me that she was always angry, always hostile, always on the offensive. Her anger was evident in her posture, her tone of voice, and her attitude.

Because things had been so tough for her growing up, she felt that she had a right to be angry. She saw the emotion as necessary to her survival. She had earned it; it had value; it was hers to keep.

In recovery, however, she began to see that her anger was not an asset at all, but a liability. "It kept me miserable," she said. "It kept people away. And it kept me stuck in the past. I knew it was time to change.

"They still call me 'The Angry Redhead,'" she added with a laugh. "But now they smile when they say it."

THOUGHT FOR TODAY· You have the right to your anger. You also have the right to the misery it brings.

Anger was our nemesis. For many of us, it still remains so. When we allow ourselves to be swept away by this turbulent emotion, it takes us to places we don't want to go.

It doesn't matter why we're angry or at whom we're angry. It doesn't matter whether we're right or wrong, or if anger is a proper response. What does matter is this: When we become enraged and lose control, we're the ones who suffer.

Our unrestrained anger can make us do irrational and hurtful things. We insult those we love; we create problems at work; we cause emotional and even physical damage. And we demean ourselves.

Afterwards we invariably feel regret, guilt, and embarrassment for the things we've said and done. We obsessively rehash our words and actions, the responses of those we've hurt, the discomfort we now feel, the strained relationships that we've created.

Upon sober reflection, it becomes crystal clear once again that uncontrolled anger causes not only pain and disharmony in our lives, but also causes us to regress spiritually and become alienated from God.

THOUGHT FOR TODAY: Anger has chain-reaction potential.

Anger

March 30

It's not easy to stay calm and collected when we've been aggravated, insulted, or provoked. However, each time we swing the club of anger at someone or something, we're the ones who end up bruised and battered. That's why self-restraint has become such an important goal in our new lives.

When we feel rage mounting within us, we take a deep breath, fold our arms—do *whatever* it takes to buy five or ten seconds. Often, that's all the time we need to decide that it's just not worth it to explode.

At that point it's wise to walk away in order to regain composure. Talking it out with someone can neutralize our volatile·emotions and help us find perspective.

It can also be helpful to try to better understand our feelings by asking such questions as these: "Why am I getting so upset about this?" "Am I really angry, or is something else going on?" Moreover, we can try to be understanding of the others involved—to see things from their point of view.

The possibility then exists to resolve the conflict in constructive ways—by communicating our feelings calmly, by stating our case effectively, and by listening receptively while others do those same things.

THOUGHT FOR TODAY: It may be difficult to practice self-restraint, but it's impossible to take back an angry outburst.

During my first year of sobriety, I was told over and over that for me there is no such thing as justifiable anger. Unlike so-called normal people, it was explained, recovering alcoholics and addicts simply can't afford the irrational behavior and emotional hangovers that follow angry outbursts.

It sounded good in principle, but I harbored reservations. If someone wronged me, I reasoned, I wasn't about to roll over and take it. (In early recovery I often pretended to agree with a concept while secretly believing that my case was different.)

On several occasions I was driven perilously close to drinking by the chain reaction of my unrestrained anger. The last time, I went so far as to buy a bottle. It was then that I finally understood. The admonition against justifiable anger was no mere slogan or ivory-tower concept, I saw. On the contrary, it was as pragmatic as could be; it was a matter of life and death.

Later on, when I explored my reservations further, I realized that in the past I had actually enjoyed my self-righteous anger. In a perverse way, it gave me a feeling of superiority over others.

THOUGHT FOR TODAY: I may be able to justify my anger, but how will I justify my relapse?

April 1

Affirmation

Today I choose to turn away from rage and all its destructive ramifications. I am unwilling to accept the consequences of unbridled anger. When I let it run free, many are harmed, but none so grievously as I am.

Today I choose to acknowledge my anger and deal with it constructively. I will not deny or repress my anger, for then it will fester within me and taint all my thoughts and actions. But neither will I let this potentially dangerous emotion run my life.

I am grateful that I can now make the right choices when anger sweeps through me. I practice self-restraint until the rush subsides. I ask God to remove my volatile feelings. I try to gain understanding of the underlying emotions that trigger my anger. I state my case calmly and encourage others to do the same, seeking compromise and resolution rather than further discord.

Because I have undergone dramatic changes in the ways I approach and deal with anger, I am able to live at peace with myself and those around me. I heed the guidance of my spiritual self and draw closer to God.

THOUGHT FOR TODAY: I have choices concerning anger. Today I will make the ones that God would have me make.

14

Spiritual Growth

God's thoughts, His will, His love, His judgments are all man's home. To think His thoughts, to choose His will, to love His loves, to judge His judgments, and thus to know that He is in us, is to be at home.

—GEORGE MACDONALD

April 2

At the bare-root beginning of recovery, many of us were off balance in one way or another. We still suffered from the trauma and abuse we had endured growing up. We were confused, alienated, and fearful of almost everything and everyone. We lacked self-worth, and found it difficult to handle things that most people take for granted.

At first it seemed unlikely that we would ever disentangle ourselves from the past, let alone become healed and begin to grow again.

But we found a way—the way of spirituality. As our faith and trust in God mounted, we no longer needed to depend only on our own limited resources when meeting life's challenges. Spiritual principles provided solutions to daily living problems that used to baffle us. As we began to extend ourselves to others, our feelings of self-pity disappeared. We were able to experience and pass along God's love.

Surprising as it may sound, some of us have become grateful for our earlier years of pain. We believe they were instrumental in leading us to our new life—a spiritual life that is more productive and joyful than we ever dreamed possible.

THOUGHT FOR TODAY: My continuing spiritual growth makes it possible for me to recover at ever-deeper levels.

We often had the feeling that we were serving time. Life was about loose ends and unfinished business—frustration, fear, and emptiness. For years we just got by.

Even after we began to develop a working faith in God, some of us continued the same pattern. There was no new structure or purpose to our lives, no new goals. We were willing to grow spiritually, but just enough to get by.

We were willing to give up such character flaws as dishonesty, jealousy, and resentment, for example, but only to the extent that they were making us really uncomfortable. Similarly, we were willing to become more kind, tolerant, and forgiving, but only to the extent that it would take some of the tension and hostility out of our relationships.

Needless to say, our lives didn't change that much. Because of our half-measures, we still were just getting by.

Eventually, we realized that if we were going to grow and flourish, we would have to raise our sights. We would have to seek spiritual progress without reservations or limitations, trying to live as our Creator would have us live.

THOUGHT FOR TODAY: Am I still just getting by?

Spiritual Growth

April 4

Spirituality—the desire to seek and do God's will—comes to each of us for different reasons and at different times in our lives. No two people acquire or experience spirituality in the same way.

To begin with, we have varied conceptions and understandings of a Higher Power, for we have been influenced and shaped in individual and unique ways. Because of our upbringing, some of us are able to be open-minded, while others may be skeptical to the point of recalcitrance. There are also those among us who are entirely ready to embrace spirituality as soon as it is presented as a solution to long-standing living problems.

In any case, it matters not who we are, where we come from, what we've done, or if we've reached the threshold of spirituality early or late in life. The only thing that does matter is whether or not we are willing to make a start.

Moreover, once we've set out on the spiritual path, it's not important how quickly or slowly we progress, or how our growth compares to that of others. We each move forward at our own pace, and in God's time.

THOUGHT FOR TODAY: We all open the door to a spiritual life with the same key—the key of willingness.

Even after I had made the gradual transition from atheism to belief in God, it was still many months before I began to truly understand spiritual principles. It took even longer to incorporate them into my life.

Those new concepts, values, and objectives were almost completely antithetical to what I had been force-fed as a child and still clung to as an adult. What did they mean by "giving to receive," "letting go and letting God," or "freedom through forgiveness"? I just couldn't get it. Often, the feeling of alienation would return—even though my friends were unfailingly supportive and patient.

For quite some time, I was too embarrassed to admit my confusion. But, as open-mindedly as I could, I did keep listening to other people's experiences. I finally realized that I wasn't all that unique in my inability to readily grasp spiritual principles. I began to ask questions.

I applied spiritual principles in small ways at first. Even though I didn't have full understanding or, for that matter, that much real faith in a particular principle, I became willing to at least try it in my life.

I don't know exactly when it all clicked, but eventually it did. And my life began to turn around.

THOUGHT FOR TODAY: You don't have to fully understand a spiritual principle before applying it— and benefiting from it.

Spiritual Growth

April 6

We embarked on a spiritual journey only to find that our destination would forever be out of reach. We realized that spiritual perfection is God's province, and all we can hope for is progress in that direction.

The excitement and reward is in the journey itself, and that is enough to keep us going. We make discoveries, experience wonder, become transformed, and feel ourselves moving closer to God. We travel from despair to gladness, from bewilderment to comprehension, from hatred to love.

This is not to say that the road is always smooth or laid out clearly before us. There are valleys, peaks, and plateaus, as well as detours and occasional landslides.

It's a fascinating reality that we often gain more ground after we make a series of wrong turns and temporarily lose our way, than when the road stretches out straight as an arrow.

Sometimes it seems that our journey is over—that we've reached a dead end. But then God shows us the way, and the road suddenly opens up in front of us once more . . . .

THOUGHT FOR TODAY: The milestones of progress on my spiritual journey are freedom, joy, serenity.

Every so often, I get discouraged about my "lack" of progress. It seems that I've just been marking time, even sliding backwards. But then, almost inevitably, I have an experience—not necessarily a dramatic one—which shows me how far I've actually come.

As a good example, a friend and I were at a baseball game. A few rows in front of us, two fans of the visiting team were noisily taunting the home team fans with shouts, gestures, and occasional obscenities.

Somewhere around the fifth inning, my friend turned to me with a wide grin on his face. "In the old days," he reminded me, "you and I would have had zero tolerance for those two idiots. We would have taken them on, and maybe even sent them flying over the railing down onto the field. And just look at us—we're hardly paying any attention to them."

We both laughed and started making additional comparisons between the past and present, realizing how far we had come. Once again, in spite of my earlier doubts about my level of personal growth, I was able to see clearly that I was indeed moving forward.

THOUGHT FOR TODAY: If you are wondering about your progress in recovery, just think back to a month ago, a year ago, five years ago.

April 8

Affirmation

The spiritual way of life has made it possible for me to become healthy and whole again. The wounds of the past have been healed, and I can freely move forward.

Before I began to grow spiritually, I lacked tools for living and, in fact, had no real idea *how* to live. Today, thanks to God, I have found a way to meet and transcend the daily challenges that used to bewilder and defeat me.

For the first time, my life has true purpose, direction, and stability. Even when I am swayed by the currents of change, my inner, spiritual self can remain undisturbed by outer circumstances. I have confidence that a strong and loving God will unerringly guide me through all experiences.

Now that I have begun to savor and appreciate the rewards of spiritual growth, just "getting by" is not enough for me. I choose to abandon limited objectives, and to seek spiritual progress without reservations. Although the goal of spiritual perfection will forever be out of reach, that does not deter me, for I have found that the joy is in the journey.

THOUGHT FOR TODAY: I am grateful that I can approach this day with purpose and confidence.

15

Blamers and Martyrs

This is the true joy in life, the being used for a purpose recognized by yourself as a mighty one; the being thoroughly worn out before you are thrown on the scrap heap; the being a force of nature instead of a feverish selfish little clod of ailments and grievances complaining that the world will not devote itself to making you happy.

—George Bernard Shaw

April 9

Personal and spiritual growth have become vivid realities in our lives. Yet for some of us, recovery and change remained out of reach for years. We just couldn't let go of identities and mind-sets rooted in the past. We were perennial victims.

By blaming childhood mistreatment—and that alone—for the problems we suffered later on, we absolved ourselves of responsibility for failed relationships, destructive behavior, addictions, and despair. In effect we gave ourselves permission not to seek solutions, not to act, not to change.

We realize now that our martyrdom, however unwitting it may have been, kept us stuck in the past while shortchanging us in other ways as well. During those years we missed out on the challenge and rewards of self-discovery and spiritual enlightenment. Instead, we poisoned ourselves with resentments and self-pity.

Unquestionably our lives have been strongly influenced and in some cases deeply damaged by past experiences. We firmly believe, however, that once we've learned what we can from the past, it's up to us to move forward and take responsibility for our lives today—working through the problems, savoring the freedom, sharing the joys.

THOUGHT FOR TODAY: When I continue to see myself as a helpless victim of the past, I victimize myself in the present.

Blamers and Martyrs   **114**

I once had a lengthy conversation with a young man who was deeply unhappy about the conditions of his life. His fervent wish was to become a professional writer, but after a few frustrating experiences he had convinced himself that he could never be successful in that occupation. He approached his relationships and financial prospects—indeed, his overall ability to fit into the world and enjoy life—in much the same way.

The young man had grown up in an alcoholic family. Although he had plenty of talent and potential, he held fast to the belief that he was the product of "bad genes" and therefore incapable of attaining success in any of life's arenas.

I tried to convince him that he had not been "born to lose." Just the opposite could be true, I told him, if only he would stop using his family background and alleged "bad genes" as an excuse to feel sorry for himself and give up.

At the time of our conversation, he was keenly aware of the influences that had shaped him. It wasn't until months later that he was able to use these insights as a starting point for a better life, rather than a way to avoid risks and stay stuck.

THOUGHT FOR TODAY: Awareness is not a stopping place, but a starting point.

April 11

During our years of feeling victimized, there were times when we shifted focus from family to God Himself. "Why is He doing this to me?" we cried. Perhaps we believed that God had singled us out for punishment. Perhaps we saw our constant adversities as His way of testing us. Or maybe we felt that He had forgotten us or completely abandoned us.

There was a supreme irony to all of this. For when we finally prayed in desperation to be relieved of our misery, it was God who showed us the way. He provided the inspiration and courage that enabled us to rise from a wasteland of self-pity into the abundance of here and now.

We have no doubt whatsoever about God's ever-loving presence in our lives today. Although we each understand Him in our own individual way, we are all equal in His sight, and we are all deserving of His care and protection. We see God not as a source of our difficulties, but as the ultimate solution to them.

THOUGHT FOR TODAY: My loving Father never tests my worthiness, but forever affirms it with His grace.

It was an automatic reflex for me to throw blame around. When I experienced frustration on the job, I blamed my supervisor or "the system." When I came home in a rotten mood, I blamed the people I lived with. When I made an error, I blamed it on bad advice, a distraction, a coworker—you name it.

When I chose a new direction and began to get well, I quickly discovered I could no longer get away with blaming others for my shortcomings and misadventures. It became necessary to take responsibility for my own emotions and actions. If I was frustrated, irritable, or had made a mistake, it was important to search within myself for the reasons and potential solutions.

Over time, I've made considerable progress in developing more mature attitudes and behavior. Today I try to admit my faults instead of pointing the finger at others. I take constructive action to right wrongs and correct errors. I promptly make amends if they are called for.

I'm not swimming upstream anymore. I'm not exhausting myself trying to justify my every action. I'm not complicating the lives of everyone around me. It's so much easier to live this way.

THOUGHT FOR TODAY: When I point a finger at someone, three fingers point back at me.

For years our relationships were largely unsuccessful. This was true not only of friendships and marriages, but also of involvements with family members, coworkers, and even neighbors.

When we take a hard look at the past, we can gain awareness of the many ways in which our self-centered behavior tainted and ruined these relationships. Our tendency toward blame-throwing and martyrdom was especially destructive.

What happens in a relationship when we avoid responsibility for a problem by blaming it on someone else? Instant polarization takes place. We are forced farther apart rather than brought closer together. Real communication is replaced with hostility, manipulation, and dishonesty.

These days when there's something that needs to be resolved in a relationship, we try to bring harmony rather than discord to the table. We ask ourselves if *we're* contributing to the problem in any way, focusing on our own behavior rather than that of others. We work to keep the lines of communication open. We try to be supportive, understanding, and caring.

We used to think it was impossible for us to have successful relationships. But that's all changed now. One of the biggest miracles of recovery is the way we get along with others.

THOUGHT FOR TODAY: My objective is to solve the problem, rather than to decide who's right and who's wrong.

To this day many of us still futilely try to please the martyrs in our lives. Even though we hate ourselves for doing so, we give power to guilt-provoking parents, partners, and employers. We're easily manipulated and all too willing to accept blame.

Examples flood to mind: The parent who harps on your lack of appreciation for sacrifices made on your behalf; the employer who ruthlessly blames you for everything that goes wrong, from machine breakdowns to tax audits; the manipulative spouse who holds you personally responsible for unfulfilled aspirations.

If we've decided that it's time to stop participating in this dance of death—that it's time to restore our dignity and self-respect—here are some realities worth examining.

No matter how much we give or give in to meet the martyr's incessant demands, it will never be enough.

Giving and accepting guilt is usually a deeply grooved pattern. It will take time, patience, and perhaps pain to change it. Moreover, it is highly unlikely that the martyr will accept our new approach without an all-out counterattack.

Perhaps most important, our goal is not to change the martyr, but to change our way of reacting and interacting.

THOUGHT FOR TODAY: Just as martyrdom is a choice, so is my willingness—or refusal—to be victimized by it.

Blamers and Martyrs

April 15

Affirmation

I believed that my past would forever cast a shadow over my present and future. I saw myself as a hapless victim, doomed to a treadmill existence. I was blind to the choices in life. I couldn't have imagined, even in my wildest dreams, how dramatically everything would change.

The experiences of the past are no longer a hindrance, but a source of valuable insights which help me meet the challenges and opportunities of each new day. My thoughts and actions are centered in the here and now.

I am responsible. When I face adversity or I am revisited by harmful emotions such as fear, guilt, and self-pity, I no longer blame others or look to them for relief. I look to myself and the power of God within me to regain composure and inner security.

These days when I am on the receiving end of a martyr's onslaught, I have clear choices. I can go on the defensive or capitulate, as I automatically did in the past, or I can state my case and refuse to play the game.

Today I choose to overcome my difficulties, rather than succumb to them. Today I choose to pursue wellness and spiritual enlightenment.

THOUGHT FOR TODAY: I am neither a martyr nor a victim. I am enlightened, responsible, and recovering.

16

Feelings

Below the surface stream, shallow and light,
Of what we say we feel—below the stream,
As light, of what we think we feel, there flows
With noiseless current, strong, obscure and deep,
The central stream of what we feel indeed.

—MATTHEW ARNOLD

April 16

Chances are that our problems with feelings began when we were very young. Some of us grew up in households where we were almost never asked, "How do you feel?" In fact, we were actively discouraged from expressing our feelings, whether they concerned minor incidents at school or something as traumatic as the death of a pet.

Or perhaps we were allowed to have only "positive" feelings; negative ones brought quick disapproval. In some cases, the chaos at home evoked such painful emotions that we censored ourselves.

Given such dysfunctional scenarios, it's no wonder that we ended up with ideas such as these: It's not acceptable to openly express feelings; it's better to hide, ignore, or misrepresent them. It's not manly or mature to be sensitive and show "inappropriate" emotions such as sadness, fear, or disappointment. It's not a good idea to let others know how you really feel; if you do, you're bound to get hurt.

In recovery, we're learning entirely different lessons about our feelings. First of all, they are an essential part of each of us. They exist and they are real. They need to be faced, expressed, embraced, changed, or worked through. Our feelings add color and dimension to what otherwise would be a flat and monochromatic world.

THOUGHT FOR TODAY: My feelings contribute to my wholeness.

Feelings

These days we're convinced that the degree to which we're in touch with our feelings has a strong bearing on our emotional and physical well-being. That's why we allow our feelings to surface; that's why we welcome them into our consciousness. Whether our feelings are exhilarating or disturbing, we give them permission to "be."

As we all know, some feelings are abstract and relatively unimportant. They come and go, like dreams. But we've found that other feelings can actually help us identify problems—usually within ourselves—that need to be faced and dealt with.

If in the past we felt depressed, for example, we likely pushed that feeling away. Today, in contrast, we let the emotion enter our awareness, we look at it honestly, and we try to discover what it's telling us about ourselves and what (if anything) needs to be done. We're not just depressed. We're depressed *because* of this, *because* of that, or for a combination of reasons.

Thankfully we no longer have to deny or be dragged along by our feelings. We can learn from them and enjoy them.

THOUGHT FOR TODAY: Whatever feelings I have today, they are "okay."

Feelings

April 18

I still remember many of the painful feelings I had as a teenager. Armies of contradictory emotions marched across the battlefield of my mind. I felt hatred for my parents, yet hungered for their love and approval. I loathed myself with suicidal zeal, yet frequently felt superior to those around me. I was self-conscious to the point of paralysis, yet longed to be noticed.

At the age of thirteen or fourteen I discovered that alcohol effectively blotted out those feelings, or at least reduced their intensity. I relied on it for many years.

When I finally quit drinking and began my recovery, the feelings I had buried came quickly back to life. They were as intense and erratic as ever. Once again my emotions were causing me pain.

Very gradually, with hard work and a lot of help from new friends, I began to identify my feelings and even to understand them. And it wasn't all an uphill climb. For years I had obliterated good feelings as well as painful ones, and I soon was able to experience joy, fascination, and excitement on a regular basis.

THOUGHT FOR TODAY: Buried feelings stay alive.

Feelings   124

Even though I quickly began to get in touch with long-repressed feelings in early recovery, it was months before I was able to express them. It was easier for me to talk about aberrant behavior and sordid experiences of the past than it was to reveal present-day emotions such as anxiety, jealousy, confusion, or frustration.

I can now see why I guarded my feelings so closely back then. For one thing, I hadn't yet learned to trust other people. I was ashamed of some of the feelings I had—and was unwilling to risk becoming vulnerable. Moreover, I was convinced that my new friends wouldn't really understand.

Not surprisingly, the longer I kept my feelings to myself the longer I dragged my feet in recovery. I continued to experience discomfort born of unexpressed emotions. And to a large extent I remained alienated from myself and those around me.

When I was able to let down my guard somewhat and reveal several especially troubling feelings, I experienced great relief. Even more encouraging, however, was the empathetic and appreciative response I received. It was a major step forward, and it set the stage for accelerated progress.

THOUGHT FOR TODAY: Sharing my feelings with those I trust is an essential ingredient in my ongoing recovery.

Feelings

April 20

We used to be at the mercy of our feelings. They controlled us, rather than the other way around. They caused us to act in extreme ways and forced us to do things we really didn't want to do.

When we felt angry, we lashed out or sought revenge. When we felt misunderstood, we withdrew from the world and sulked for days. When we felt disappointed in ourselves, we behaved self-destructively. To make matters worse, when we had painful feelings we tended to hang on to them interminably.

Times have changed for us. We no longer are willing to endure suffering and pain at the behest of our emotions. Although we still experience many of the same feelings we used to, we're not tyrannized by them for weeks. In addition, we're better able to take responsibility—to work through our feelings, to get rid of them, to let them go and let them change.

Best of all, we have choices. We don't have to act out negative feelings in destructive ways anymore. We're not locked into our feelings, especially if they are inappropriate and out of step with the new cadence of our lives.

THOUGHT FOR TODAY: I don't have to hang on to emotions that cause me harm.

"I had a lot of feelings I refused to admit, even to myself," a friend told me. "When one of those feelings came up, I would disguise it as something else. If I felt uncomfortable in a crowd, for instance, I might convince myself that I was bored, or that the other people were all idiots."

I knew exactly what he meant, because for years I had done the same thing myself. It was as if my feelings had been divided into two categories—acceptable and unacceptable. "Whenever there was a holiday," I said, "I convinced myself that I hated it—because it was too commercial, because people were phony, because of those obligatory family get-togethers, and so on. What I was really feeling, of course, was alienation, painful memories, depression—you know."

We agreed that as long as we continued to disguise our feelings, we denied ourselves the opportunity to work through them. Once we began to honestly look at our true emotions—no matter what they were—and deal with them constructively, then we were able to climb out of the ruts we had dug, to experience life in entirely new ways, and to be a lot more comfortable with ourselves.

THOUGHT FOR TODAY: If I become irritable, bored, or impatient today, I will ask myself what I am really feeling.

April 22

Affirmation

I celebrate my feelings. They are real, vital, and as much a part of me as my physical being. They add vibrancy and depth to my life.

I allow each and every emotion to freely surface and enter my consciousness. For I know with certainty that if I were to deny, disguise, or attempt to obliterate any feeling, I would give up a valuable part of my wholeness.

I embrace all of my feelings without judgment. They are neither acceptable nor unacceptable, neither appropriate nor inappropriate, neither right nor wrong. They simply are.

I express my feelings to others. By sharing them and comparing them openly and honestly, I gain fellowship, relief, and understanding.

I approach my feelings as allies rather than enemies. They help me see the truths of my inner and outer worlds. They let me know when and where I must change.

I have no fear that my joyful feelings will slip away too quickly, or that my unpleasant ones will linger indefinitely. My emotions are the currents of my life.

THOUGHT FOR TODAY: I view my feelings not with fear but with expectation; not with shame but with acceptance; not with avoidance but with gratitude.

Feelings   128

17

Open-mindedness

There are boxes in the mind with labels on them: To study on a favorable occasion; Never to be thought about; Useless to go into further; Contents unexamined; Pointless business; Urgent; Dangerous; Delicate; Impossible; Abandoned; Reserved; For others; My forte; etc.

—PAUL VALÉRY

April 23

"Don't take this the wrong way," the man said to me. He had asked for a lift home after a meeting of my new recovery group. I shrugged and waited for him to continue.

"I've been listening to you lately," he went on, "and you seem to have this contemptuous reaction to what other people say. You're probably not even aware of it."

I felt like pulling over and telling him to get out of the car, but then he said something that settled me down. "I'm telling you this because I used to be just like you. I heard what people said, but I didn't want to listen. I spun my wheels for six months.

"Try to remember that your ideas are what got you here," he told me carefully. "*Your* ideas and *your* way of doing things were *your* downfall. If you want to get well you're going to have to open up your mind to new ideas and new ways."

Maybe he was right, I thought later. I remembered how "one-way" I'd always been—drinking, fighting, arguing, rebelling. I could see myself flailing away at the world without rhyme or reason. Maybe he was right . . . .

THOUGHT FOR TODAY: Listen to learn, and learn to listen.

We're beginning to see that our closed-mindedness was more than an arbitrary approach to life, existing in and of itself. It was comprised of attitudes we had developed as children, along with specific character defects. There was more to our closed-mindedness than met the eye.

Very often, our unwillingness to consider new ideas reflected a need to deny the reality of what was going on around us, or within us. If a parent was a practicing alcoholic, for example, we refused to acknowledge his or her illness and all its destructive ramifications. We closed our minds to the entire subject of addiction.

In other dysfunctional family situations, negative emotions may have brought about closed-mindedness. If we were victims of physical or sexual abuse, it is likely that fear, shame, and guilt kept our minds closed—not only to the truth of what was taking place, but to the possibility that help was available.

Or perhaps our closed-mindedness was the result of egocentricity—the self-centered illusion that the universe revolved around us and we "knew it all."

When we think back to those attitudes and that way of life, that's when we're especially grateful for our new and growing open-mindedness.

THOUGHT FOR TODAY: When I am closed-minded, I resist change even when it is urgently required.

April 25

We've learned a lot, and for the most part we've been successful at applying what we've learned. The despair we once felt has lifted, and we're starting to enjoy ourselves. Our relationships are improving, we're getting along well at work, and we usually know what to do when we have problems. Just about everything has begun to turn around for us.

But are we staying teachable? Are we continuing to listen and learn with the same open-mindedness that has served us so well up to this point? Perhaps we've begun to feel that we've learned enough, that our momentum by itself will keep us moving forward.

Those of us who have fallen into this trap know from experience that it can lead to retrogression. When we shut our minds to the ideas and suggestions of other people, a feeling of apartness frequently sets in. When we stop searching for new levels of understanding, we're in danger of slipping back to our old ways—of becoming pessimistic, fearful, and angry.

But if we stay teachable we almost certainly will continue to grow. There will be no boundaries to the potential depth and breadth of our spiritual development, and to the richness of our lives.

THOUGHT FOR TODAY: I will live my life to the fullest. I will stay receptive to new ideas.

When we cultivate open-mindedness, each day has the rich potential for new experiences, new activities, new ideas, new pleasures. The more open-minded we are, the more appreciative we can be of the abundance with which we have been blessed.

We've begun to see life as a process of continuing growth and change; more is constantly being revealed and offered. Because of our open-mindedness, we've become receptive to special joys and discoveries we might otherwise have missed.

By listening attentively to the views and visions of others, we have been able to expand our own horizons. We experience the world around us in an entirely new way. No person, no structure, no creation, no form of nature is without interest; there is always something for us to learn.

As our minds open wider to the reality of God, we become increasingly conscious of His love and His desire to bring good into our lives. That good may come to us through unexpected channels and in seemingly unlikely ways, but we are open and trusting that God will always provide for us in the right way at the right time.

THOUGHT FOR TODAY: Open-mindedness allows me to experience the world in an entirely new way.

Open-mindedness

April 27

We never thought of ourselves as intolerant. On the contrary, we had always taken pride in our "democratic" approach to our neighbors, those with whom we worked, and even strangers or newcomers.

It was only when we began living spiritual lives and gradually became more open-minded that we realized how intolerant we had actually been.

The targets of our intolerance of course varied for each of us, but in general the thrust was the same. We were intolerant of people who didn't share our aspirations, who had unsophisticated tastes, who moved around a lot. We were intolerant of people whose approach to life differed radically from our own, who were willing to settle for less, who stayed in one place, who had a different view of faith. We were intolerant of people who were intolerant . . . .

It's clear to us today that intolerance breeds discord—and our goal is to live in harmony and brotherhood. Intolerance means judgmentalism—and our goal is to become more accepting. Intolerance keeps us on edge—and our goal is serenity. Intolerance is closed-mindedness—and our goal is open-mindedness.

THOUGHT FOR TODAY: My intolerance harms no one as seriously as it harms me.

I once heard a man describe his ten-year struggle to overcome alcoholism and drug addiction. He had been in and out of countless detoxification centers, treatment facilities, and hospitals. He would sober up while he was inside, but would invariably get loaded within days following his release.

"After a while I thought that was the way my life had to be, that there was no hope for someone like me," he said. "I couldn't figure out why I was having such a hard time."

He had been clean and sober for several years, and someone in the room asked him what had happened to turn things around.

"The last time, whatever they told me to do, I did," he responded. "I didn't think about it, analyze it, question it, or change it to suit me. I just went ahead and did it. And here I am.

"Before, if someone suggested something, my mind would snap shut. I thought I was different, but I was just being stubborn. If you told me to go right, I'd go left. I kept doing that until I ended up in a skid row alley with my head bashed in. That's when I decided it was time to listen."

THOUGHT FOR TODAY: When I'm open-minded, I don't have to learn things the hard way.

Open-mindedness

April 29

Affirmation

Open-mindedness has expanded my vision of the world, allowing me to experience life in ways that were hitherto impossible. I value my openness and the abundance it brings. When barriers such as fear, denial, or egocentricity threaten to restrict my new vision, I will act quickly to break them down.

I welcome change. I am receptive to new ideas, new ways, new suggestions. Life is so much easier now that I am open-minded. I can benefit from the wisdom and experience of my fellows and no longer have to learn the hard way.

As long as I remain teachable, there are no limits to the potential depth and breadth of my spiritual development. No matter how far I've come, how comfortable I feel, or how rich and joyous my life has become, I can always learn more and go farther.

Because I try to approach each new day with an openness of mind and spirit, I am more likely to be kind, understanding, and patient with myself and others—and less likely to be uncaring, judgmental, and intolerant.

THOUGHT FOR TODAY: When I am open-minded to new solutions, I can deal more effectively with new challenges.

18

Tools of Self-discovery

'Tis greatly wise to talk with our own hearts, and ask them how we stand toward God and heaven; where we have failed; and how we may avoid failure in future; how grow wise and good; how others, bless, and be ourselves approved, by God, and conscience, and our fellow-men.

—EDWARD YOUNG

April 30

Before I got sober I stayed as far away as I could from the mine field of self-knowledge. Everything I had ever found out about myself had caused me pain, it seemed. Besides, I thought I already knew all I needed to know. The truth was that I knew almost nothing.

That all turned around during my early involvement with other recovering people. To my astonishment, they talked openly about their feelings, fears, and personal discoveries. Little by little my mind opened, and I began to learn about myself from them.

I had overflowed with rage all of my life, but only by listening to others did I begin to understand causes, effects, and solutions for my anger. My hatred for people and institutions had eaten away at me for years, but it was only in recovery that I learned what resentment was—and that it could destroy me. I had always been tormented by obsessions, but only in recovery did I learn how to deal with them.

Self-discovery remains a rich and ongoing process for me. Because I continue to listen and relate to others, new truths and revelations keep coming my way. Hopefully, I will never stop learning.

THOUGHT FOR TODAY: When someone shares personal experience, strength, and hope with me, I will listen in order to learn.

Tools of Self-discovery   138

One of the most practical and revealing tools of self-discovery is a written personal inventory. By fearlessly and thoroughly surveying our past and present, we can unearth the personality traits that are blocking our progress, while also bringing to light those worth cultivating.

We take an inventory to get a clear picture of who we are and where we stand in the world. We try to identify and probe such character defects as selfishness, immaturity, dishonesty, and judgmentalism. By doing this, we learn how these flaws manifest themselves in our lives and contribute to our unhappiness. For example, many of us are able to see for the first time the extent to which self-pity has held us back, or that we've been completely dependent on other people for our security and sense of well-being.

An inventory is a personal house-cleaning of sorts, which enables us to finally get rid of our secrets and sweep away the wreckage of the past. It also serves as a road map for future action and correction, as well as a baseline against which we can measure progress. Most importantly, it leads us from pride toward humility while bringing us closer to ourselves, to others, and to God.

THOUGHT FOR TODAY: It's time for me to find out who I really am. It's time to write a personal inventory.

May 2

Now that you have a solid foothold in recovery, you're ready to take a personal inventory—to dig deeper and find out more about yourself. But perhaps you're afraid to get started. You're not sure what to write about, what method to use, or how detailed your inventory should be.

At this point it's important to remember that you're writing an inventory to grow personally and spiritually. Keeping those goals in mind, it will be a lot easier to figure out the best ways to proceed.

Some people list long-standing resentments and their causes, then turn their eyes inward to see how their own behavior contributed to the conflicts. To gain further understanding of the patterns blocking their progress, others also write extensively about their fears, feelings, and character defects.

Another important purpose of an inventory is to expose and become free of all your secrets. The relief you'll experience in "coming clean" will likely far outweigh all of your previous apprehensions.

When you sit down to write your self-survey, don't forget that it's a tool for self-discovery; it's not meant for self-flagellation. So it's just as important to explore your assets as it is your liabilities.

THOUGHT FOR TODAY: I will aim for honesty, thoroughness, and balance in my inventory. For I will get out of it what I put into it.

Many of us balked at the idea of reading our inventory to another person. We were ashamed and embarrassed at some of the things we had to admit. "What's the point?" we protested defensively.

The point is further personal and spiritual growth, we were told. When we unload our secrets and admit our character defects to another person and God, we make a big start at gaining humility, our friends emphasized. And we soon discovered that they were absolutely right—that it was just as revealing and beneficial to share our inventory as it was to write it.

For one thing, we benefited from the feedback we received. Our confidante was extremely helpful in pointing out patterns, defects, and assets we couldn't see on our own. Since we had chosen the person carefully, he or she not only understood us because of similar personal experiences, but was able to offer specific solutions.

In addition, practically every one of us found out we weren't as "bad" or "sick" as we thought we were. We gained an unexpected sense of fellowship from finally trusting another person at such a deep level. For many of us, this was the first time we were able to forgive ourselves.

THOUGHT FOR TODAY: Am I still trying to carry the load alone?

May 4

I had heard nothing but good things from people who had written and shared personal inventories. That's what finally made me want to do it. Although I was reluctant, once I got started I couldn't stop. It was as if a dam had broken inside of me. Feelings, shortcomings, and past wrongs that I had denied, forgotten, or held back for years flooded into my notebook.

I read my inventory to a trusted friend, and for the first time completely owned up to my damaging attitudes and behavior. In an almost revelationary way I was able to see the extent of my hunger for approval, and the depth and breadth of fear in my life.

While I was enormously relieved, I was also overwhelmed by the many changes that needed to be made. And I knew with certainty that it would be impossible to bring about those changes on my own.

Because of that realization, I became willing to ask for God's help in getting rid of my character defects—and doing whatever else might be necessary to grow spiritually. Looking back, it's clear that writing and sharing a personal inventory were important steps forward in faith.

THOUGHT FOR TODAY: Just because I admit my faults doesn't mean I'm stuck with them.

Tools of Self-discovery   142

May 5

Our discoveries about ourselves come from many sources—from soul-searching, from reading, and from interaction with other people. Perhaps the most overlooked source, however, is the spiritual wellspring we find within ourselves.

On occasion we are provided with important and even profound insights when we least expect them. Most of the time, though, God's wisdom comes to us when we're in a receptive frame of mind.

How can we clear the spiritual channel to better know ourselves? Naturally, each of us finds his or her own special way. Some people periodically go on retreats devoted to inner reflection and spiritual development. Others set aside time each day to strengthen their contact with the God of their own understanding. Still others make it a practice to regularly spend time in the place where they feel closest to God.

We take these actions in order to build our relationship with God and, through His grace, to learn more about ourselves. Along the way we receive other benefits as well. We receive guidance to help us make the right decisions in our lives. We achieve peace of mind. We further our progress in recovery.

THOUGHT FOR TODAY: In my search for self-knowledge, I will pay special attention to the spiritual voice within.

May 6

Affirmation

Just when I think I have reached a plateau on my spiritual journey, I am led to challenging new terrain.

When I look back it is gratifying to see the many peaks and valleys I have already crossed. What means even more are the ever-deepening levels of self-knowledge I have gained along the way.

Getting in touch with my inner self by identifying and sharing with others has brought about the death of alienation and the birth of fellowship.

Exploring every corner of my past and present with a fearless self-survey has provided me with a road map for future action and correction.

Admitting the truths I have discovered, and the secrets I have uncovered, has brought relief that is indescribable. Unburdening myself to another person and to God has opened wide the door to trust and self-forgiveness.

Because of the many ways self-discovery has thus far enriched my life, I look forward with great anticipation to what lies ahead. I look forward to new frontiers and new horizons.

THOUGHT FOR TODAY: There are no boundaries to self-discovery, nor are there limits to its rewards.

19

Success and Achievement

Why should we be in such desperate haste to succeed, and in such desperate enterprises? If a man does not keep pace with his companions, perhaps it is because he hears a different drummer.

—HENRY DAVID THOREAU

May 7

My old sensibilities about success and achievement come embarrassingly to mind when I recall a job I once held at a magazine. I rose quickly in the organization and was soon writing cover stories. I received a raise and was promoted to assistant editor.

My success went straight to my head. I demanded and received more raises and increasingly prestigious titles—associate editor, senior editor, management editor. Finally, I insisted that an entirely new title be created for me: senior management editor. That way, I would be listed on the masthead above all the other editors and second only to the editor-in-chief.

I understand now why I behaved so childishly. One might say that I was an egomaniac with an inferiority complex. I saw myself as a star, yet deep down I believed I was a fraud—that I couldn't really write. Those feelings pressed me to demand ever-greater recognition. Yet the more I received, the wider grew the gap between my "star billing" and my low self-esteem. The pressure I generated for myself was enormous.

All of that has changed, thank God. Today I know what I am and what I'm not, and for the most part it's okay with me.

THOUGHT FOR TODAY: I am not my job, I am not my bank account. I am what is inside of me.

Even in the early stages of self-discovery, we began to recognize and talk about fears we never knew we had. When others shared about their fear of people, rejection, or failure, we identified with and tried to benefit from their experiences.

But fear of *success*? It took us a while to swallow that one. Gradually, however, we began to see patterns along those lines in our behavior. And we started to explore why it was difficult to accept the good that came our way.

We were afraid that our good fortune wasn't real—that it would disappear as quickly as it had come. We feared we wouldn't be able to "live up to" our success. We were afraid of change, especially the prospect of having to give up our life-long identities as "unsuccessful" people. Above all we believed subconsciously that we didn't deserve success.

When our fears of success flare up these days, we ask God to remove them and help us to remain grateful. As time has passed and our understanding has deepened, most of those negative feelings and inappropriate reactions have lessened in intensity. We've become more trusting of God, and better able to accept His blessings.

THOUGHT FOR TODAY: In God's eyes I am worthy of the good that comes my way.

Success and Achievement

May 9

We were totally unaware of the fact, but we had been programmed at an early age to sabotage any success or good fortune that might come our way. We carried out our mission with a variety of techniques, some of them subtle and some of them crashingly obvious.

We convinced ourselves that things weren't as good as they seemed when we found a rent-controlled apartment in a good neighborhood, for example, or when we received a windfall of some kind. We behaved inappropriately when our career or financial status took a sharp turn for the better; one day we were arrogant, the next we were self-deprecating. We sabotaged personal relationships just when they were blossoming into something special.

For most of us, our negative response to success was a reflection of low self-esteem. Because we felt unworthy, we simply couldn't accept the good things.

Now that we've discovered these vital truths about ourselves, we don't automatically shift into the "search and destroy" mode when we sense that something beneficial is about to take place in our lives. We've learned how to override those obsolete messages that tell us we're undeserving.

THOUGHT FOR TODAY: I will give up the role of saboteur. I will take my successes and achievements in stride.

In one way or another, we all did it. We set out to acquire status, money, possessions, power. Our cherished goals included a certain position, a dream house, or a special car.

Many of us worked hard and sacrificed a lot. It was extremely important to achieve those objectives, because they represented our ideals of success.

If our efforts paid off and we became "winners," we were elated. Inevitably, though, the elation subsided. We realized with dismay that nothing in our lives had really changed. We had the same concerns, fears, and uncertainties. We felt as insecure and unhappy as before.

We had to go through the cycle more than once to realize that we were seeking success in places where it couldn't be found. We learned—and we've had to relearn again and again—that real success has little to do with outside things and everything to do with inside things.

We still try to improve our lot in life, but without the illusion that material achievements are synonymous with succeeding or winning. We became true winners when we finally were willing to be ourselves—when spiritual enlightenment and inner peace became our primary goals.

THOUGHT FOR TODAY: I will set my sights on inner success.

Success and Achievement

May 11

When I was still drinking, my personal triumphs were almost always followed and overshadowed by monumental binges. Even though I knew alcohol was a serious problem, I had no idea that such a predictable pattern of self-destruction existed in my life. I was completely unaware that deeply ingrained messages compelled me to act as I did.

My parents had taught me that I was unworthy of success and incapable of achieving it. For years I tried to prove that message wrong, but invariably succumbed by pulling the house down around me just as soon as I had it built.

Typically, I would work hard for a raise, a promotion, a down payment—whatever. When I finally achieved the goal, it was only a matter of hours before I was on a drunk that could last for days. Even in early sobriety, my successes were frequently followed by damaging emotional benders.

Today those childhood messages have lost most of their power. Moreover, achievement and personal triumph have far different meanings than they used to. Each day I try to do what's put in front of me. If success comes my way, I am grateful; if it doesn't, that's all right too.

THOUGHT FOR TODAY: I am worthy and deserving of good. I will put aside the negative messages of the past.

As we've progressed spiritually, our beliefs about success and achievement have changed dramatically. Each of us is unique in God's eyes. We have come from different backgrounds, are led along different paths, and have individual destinies.

That being the case, what standards do we apply to determine who is successful and who is not? What sort of measuring stick can we use to gauge achievement? Clearly, what constitutes success for one person may not be success for another.

We used to believe that a person had "arrived" if he or she had achieved certain material goals. Today we believe that the joy is in the journey, that successes come along the way, that there is no ending.

We are less driven and more flexible in our pursuit of material goals today, because our overriding objective is to seek and do God's will. If we find that our goals are not harmonious or in accord with His plan for us, we are free to modify or discard them.

If success comes to us, we try to accept it with humility. For we have come to believe that any successes we have are more God's doing than our own.

THOUGHT FOR TODAY: My life is successful because of my trust in God and my willingness to do His will.

May 13

I hold to the truth that God's loving spirit is forever present, leading me to prosperity and abundance. I affirm that I am fully deserving and worthy of the successes He has brought into my life. If thoughts to the contrary enter my mind, I will see them for the falsehoods they are.

When good fortune or personal triumphs occur, I will be accepting and grateful. I will make neither too much nor too little of my successes, but will try to take them in stride. I will not question God's gifts, nor my ability to put them to productive use.

I will keep material pursuits in perspective, for my progress cannot be measured solely by income or possessions. While these things may be part of my prosperity, the more important parts are spiritual qualities such as character building, patience, kindness, and generosity.

In order to show my appreciation to God for my successes and achievements, I will use my talents and abilities to the fullest. I will try to add happiness and fulfillment not only to my own life, but to the lives of others.

THOUGHT FOR TODAY: Success is God's gift to me. How I accept it and what I do with it are my gifts to Him.

20

Prayer and Meditation

Sometimes, perhaps, thou hearest another pray with much freedom and fluency, whilst thou canst hardly get out a few broken words. Hence thou art ready to accuse thyself and admire him, as if the gilding of the key made it open the door the better.

—WILLIAM GURNALL

May 14

For countless millions of people throughout history, prayer and meditation have been the pathway to inner strength. The very same is true for us. No matter where we may be, what we may be doing, or what challenges we may face, prayer and meditation can bring us guidance, serenity, and a sense of closeness with our Higher Power.

Prayer is the way we "talk" to God. It is the means by which we communicate our thoughts, emotions, desires, fears, and gratitude. Perhaps most important, prayer is our way of asking what He would have us do and be. We don't know if prayer changes God, but we do know without question that it changes us.

Meditation is the way we "listen" to God. When we meditate, we retreat from the physical and emotional distractions of the outside world. In a manner of our own choosing, we seek direction from God as we understand Him.

Many of us had long believed that God existed, but it was not until we began to pray and meditate that our belief was concretized. Today, because of prayer and meditation, we truly feel the presence of God in our lives.

THOUGHT FOR TODAY: Prayer and meditation are my means of personal communication with God.

I spent many years disclaiming the purpose and power of prayer. When I finally did begin to pray, it was not with a great deal of spiritual enlightenment. In truth, I was still quite skeptical. My attitude was, "What do I have to lose?"

In retrospect, a far more appropriate question would have been, "What do I have to *gain*?"

Through prayer, I've found assurance that God is far more than a nebulous force in the universe, or a creation of people's imaginations. I've been able to develop what I feel is a personal relationship with Him, a sense of closeness and even intimacy.

Because I have sought God's guidance and partnership through prayer, remarkable changes have taken place in my life. When I have humbly asked Him to remove my fears, obsessions, resentments, and other troubling character defects, He has done so.

When something calamitous or simply unforeseen throws me off balance, prayer is always a safe harbor. When I turn to God at such times, I become stabilized and reassured.

Through prayer, I reaffirm that I am a child of God—that I am never alone, that He is always at hand to protect and care for me.

THOUGHT FOR TODAY: Thank you, God, for this day, your presence, and the power of every prayer.

When we practice meditation on a regular basis, we find we're more sensitive and receptive to God's guidance. That's exactly why we meditate in the first place—to gain awareness of His will for us.

Each of us can choose our own method of meditation; there is no right or wrong way to listen for God's guidance. Some people, for example, light a candle and focus on its radiance. Others visualize a special location, or imagine themselves as an empty vessel ready to be filled.

Some of us need to meditate alone, in our own surroundings. Others feel closest to God in a place of worship such as a church, shrine, or temple.

We all find meditation especially comforting when we've arrived at a crossroads of some kind, and rely on God to show us the way. Sometimes His guidance comes immediately, during the actual meditation. At other times, hours, days, even weeks may pass, and then we may be influenced by a compelling thought or feeling.

There are still other times when God's message isn't clear, or doesn't seem to come at all. Then we try to act *as if* He is guiding us, trusting whatever instinct or inclination we may have gained through our meditation.

THOUGHT FOR TODAY: God knows the answer before I pose the question; He knows what I need before I ask Him.

"I'd like more than anything to be consistent with prayer," a friend was saying, sharing an experience common to many people. "But there are times when I drift away from God. When that happens, it doesn't seem too important, but afterwards I pay a price.

"Here's an example," she continued. "A couple of weeks ago I went skiing. We headed to the mountain early every morning, skied all day, then went out at night. By the time I got back to the room I was dead tired. I didn't even think about praying.

"After I got home, I started having problems with my mother. She's been ill, plus we haven't been getting along at all. I wanted to pray about it, but it was really hard getting started again. I felt guilty and hypocritical. I had this feeling that God was upset with me because I'd been giving Him short shrift.

"Of course, that wasn't true at all," my friend added. "*I* was the one who was upset with me. God never holds back, even when I do. Next time I start thinking I'm too busy for Him, I'll try to remember that He's never too busy for me."

THOUGHT FOR TODAY: God's love for me is strong, consistent, and abiding.

May 18

The practice of prayer and meditation has become a vital part of our lives. Without it, we would feel lost and empty. Yet ironically, when we first considered trying prayer and meditation, many of us were reluctant to begin. Most often, it was fear that held us back.

What were we afraid of? Because of our low self-esteem, we were afraid that God wouldn't want to be bothered by us. Because we lacked experience, we were afraid that we wouldn't do it right. Because of our difficulty in dealing with emotions, we were afraid to become vulnerable. Because of our upbringing, we were afraid of God Himself.

However, since we couldn't long ignore the evidence of God's power in our lives and the lives of others, we eventually overcame our reluctance. We tentatively reached out to God, and our fears soon disappeared.

Prayer and meditation is an entirely personal and individual process—that was one of our most important discoveries. We need not be concerned about using the "right" method, words, or format. God already knows what is in our hearts and minds; He understands us better than we understand ourselves.

THOUGHT FOR TODAY: When I pray, I only need an honest and open heart.

I used to dread visiting my parents, because I never knew what to expect from them. Judging from past experiences, it was more than likely that I would be verbally assaulted in some way, even if the occasion was a holiday, birthday, or anniversary.

As my faith grew during recovery, the practice of prayer and meditation helped make those visits a lot more tolerable. My communication with God enabled me to focus on the solutions instead of wallowing self-destructively in the problems.

I learned to ask God for help in accepting my parents as they were; for help in becoming more understanding and patient; for help in being forgiving; for help in practicing self-restraint.

Before leaving my home to visit my parents, or before picking up the telephone to call them, I usually took the time to pray and meditate so as to fortify myself with spiritual strength. When it was time to head for their place, or to make the phone call, I had the feeling that God was right there with me, directing my thoughts and actions, making sure that I was centered and free of fear.

THOUGHT FOR TODAY: Before I face any challenge, I will put first things first and get in touch with God.

Affirmation

Through prayer and meditation, I am drawn ever closer to God in a loving relationship that inspires and sustains me. My quiet time with Him prepares me for the day ahead. I am peaceful and poised.

It is deeply comforting to know that I can always turn to God; there are no limitations. No matter where I am, what I am doing, or what difficulties I may face, His presence assures me that good will prevail.

When I communicate with God by praying and meditating, I perceive my circumstances and relationships in a new light, and envision new possibilities. With God as my source of wisdom and strength, I focus on solutions rather than problems.

God understands me better than I understand myself. He knows what I need and when I need it before I ask Him. So it matters little what words or method I choose when I pray and meditate. He is always in my heart.

Today when I ask God what He would have me do and be, I will also take the time to express gratitude to Him for all the blessings I have received.

THOUGHT FOR TODAY: I will turn from discouragement to thoughts of God's greatness.

21

Becoming Independent

To know what you prefer, instead of humbly saying Amen to what the world tells you you ought to prefer, is to have kept your soul alive.

—Robert Louis Stevenson

Our growing independence is a sure sign we've found a way of life that really works. We've certainly come a long way from our days of chronic neediness and dependence, and we're deeply grateful.

Many of us leaned on people—parents, friends, spouses—to fill our emotional, financial, and even intellectual needs. We depended on professionals and institutions to take care of us and make us right. Perhaps we also relied on alcohol, drugs, or behavioral dependencies such as compulsive overeating to get by.

We deplored these traits in ourselves. Each time we called on someone to lend us money, bail us out, put us back together, or do what we were afraid to do, we felt ashamed. What little self-esteem we started with eroded even further over time.

Gradually, and not without difficulty, we began to break away from our limiting dependence on people, places, and things. With the help of God and the encouragement of others, we learned to take responsibility and make our own decisions—to become self-supporting in the broadest sense. Each time we took even a small step forward, it was a big boost for our self-esteem.

THOUGHT FOR TODAY: I really like the independent person I'm becoming.

Becoming Independent

I used to think of myself as a loner—self-sufficient and independent not only from relatives, friends, and coworkers, but from society as a whole. As far as I was concerned, I didn't need "nothing from nobody."

Now that I have matured somewhat, it's obvious to me that my former perception of myself was off by one hundred eighty degrees. I may have appeared to be self-reliant, but in reality I was dependent on others for emotional and physical sustenance of all kinds.

In order to win the admiration and prestige I craved, for example, I was a consummate barroom liar. In accordance with my mood or your gullibility, I could be a test pilot, a brain surgeon, or a professional athlete. If I needed to be consoled and comforted when things weren't going my way, I relied on you to come through for me. More than anything, I depended on you for approval; when it was withheld I was crushed.

What I've found over the years is that it's impossible to acquire a true sense of security and emotional well-being through the actions and good intentions of others. Those needs can only be filled from within myself, and from the God of my understanding.

THOUGHT FOR TODAY: When I count on others for security, approval, and prestige, I'm expecting too much of them and too little of myself.

Becoming Independent

May 23

"I got married the first time when I was eighteen," a friend recounted to me. "It was my way of running away from home, because I just couldn't take the sick games and fighting anymore.

"I was insecure and full of fear, with a lot of empty spaces inside," he added. "I felt my new wife could fill them in. The marriage didn't last."

My friend's second marriage followed the same pattern. This time, it seemed that his neediness—for motivation, inspiration, guidance, love—would be better filled by a house, a child, and social status. Needless to say he went through a second divorce.

In a recovery group, he eventually found out that the problem was not incompatibility or "poor choices," as he had thought, but his dependency on others to make him whole. His dysfunctional upbringing had left him with a host of unresolved conflicts and emotional deficiencies, and he expected to be rounded out by the women he had married.

"I'm not happy that my marriages broke up," my friend concluded. "But I've had a chance to work on my dependency. Little by little I'm becoming my own person, and I'm glad of that."

THOUGHT FOR TODAY: I can improve my relationships by focusing on giving rather than receiving.

Becoming Independent   **164**

We know it's not possible to find emotional well-being through dependence on another person. Similarly, we know it's not within our power to "fix" someone else. Yet we still fall into those traps from time to time.

Let's say we're involved with a person who has become overly dependent on us. What's the probable outcome?

In the first place, it's likely we'll get carried away by the power we're given in the relationship. Chances are we'll play into the other person's neediness by becoming controlling, manipulative, or even domineering. Sooner or later, our partner will rebel and turn on us.

Or suppose the situation is reversed. We're in an emotionally vulnerable state, and start relying heavily on someone to make everything all right for us. Where will it lead?

When we expect too much from another person, they're bound to fail us. And we're bound to end up feeling frustrated and disappointed. Worse, we lose the opportunity to solve our own problems, to grow, and to find strength and wholeness within ourselves.

While we're not afraid today to ask for and give support, encouragement, and love, we're careful not to become overly dependent, or to allow others to become overly dependent on us.

THOUGHT FOR TODAY: It takes two for a dependent relationship to get off the ground. I will resist the temptation to participate.

Becoming Independent

In order to find self-confidence and inner security, it was suggested, we would do well to give up our dependence on people, places, and things, and begin to depend on God.

Some of us found this idea hard to take. Now that we had come to realize how dependent we'd been all of our lives, the last thing we wanted was a *new* dependence, especially a seemingly abstract one. Or perhaps we felt that dependence on God would be a sign of weakness; after all, we were trying to become more self-reliant and *stronger*.

Even if we thought we could benefit by depending on God, we hadn't yet developed the kind of trust that would allow us to be truly comfortable with the idea. Would He come through for us?

Once we got over our initial skepticism, we were able to make the concept part of our lives one day at a time. When we were afraid, we found courage and strength by relying on God. When we were confused or indecisive, we looked to Him first for answers. When we needed something, we prayed for His guidance and help. Over the years, we've found that dependence on God is the way to true independence.

THOUGHT FOR TODAY: Dependence on God is not a sign of weakness but a source of strength.

Becoming Independent

Like so many others, I came into recovery with unmet dependency needs that kept me bound to a father and mother who no longer were in my life. Well into adulthood, I searched desperately for the love, attention, and approval they had been incapable of providing. I remained always needy and always hopeful.

It took quite some time for me to realize that the "needy child" approach to life is self-defeating. For one thing, no outside person could ever fully satisfy my tremendous emotional demands. Moreover, so long as I depended on others for my security, I would be hard pressed to provide it or develop it for myself.

It was a major challenge to finally become emotionally independent, to give up those false hopes that tied me to the past. I had to stop believing that my important needs and wants would go unfulfilled so long as they were not met by others. I had to prove that I could indeed fill many of those needs. I had to give myself permission to look within for love and approval.

THOUGHT FOR TODAY: I can achieve the goal of emotional independence by developing my inner resources.

Becoming Independent

Affirmation

I cherish my growing independence. More and more I reach within myself and toward God for a sense of wholeness and inner security. I know with certainty that my empty spaces cannot be filled and my rough edges cannot be smoothed from the outside.

I am grateful for a deeper understanding of dependency, of its sometimes subtle manifestations and impacts in my life. That understanding has brought the opportunity for action, and gradual but dynamic change.

Because I have worked to give up my dependencies on people, places, and things, I am able to do much more for myself. I am able to be responsible, to make my own decisions, to be self-supporting in all ways, to choose and pursue the path that is right for me.

Day by day my self-esteem rises. Where my former neediness caused discomfort and even shame, my newfound independence is a source of pride and satisfaction.

Today there is only one dependence with which I am comfortable—dependence on God. I have found that He is an eternal and unwavering source of guidance, courage, and strength.

THOUGHT FOR TODAY: My needs for emotional security are being met in the best ways possible—from within and from God.

Becoming Independent   **168**

22

Self-awareness

The height of all philosophy is to know thyself; and the end of this knowledge is to know God. Know thyself, that thou may knowest God; and know God, that thou mayest love Him and be like Him. In the one thou art initiated into wisdom; and in the other perfected in it.

—FRANCIS QUARLES

May 28

There's no question that our expanding self-awareness is having a powerful impact on our lives. We're discovering who we are, why we're like that, and what will help us change and grow.

We were somewhat aware of ourselves in the past, but our beliefs and perceptions tended to be erroneous and painful. If we had insights, they often became obsessions. If we recognized damaging character traits, we ignored them, denied them, or disguised them. In actuality we were self-conscious and self-centered—not self-*aware*.

Today just the opposite is true. We're making self-awareness a major priority, and it is paying off handsomely. By getting to know ourselves better, we've become more secure and less vulnerable to outside pressures—as well as our own self-destructive tapes. We're off the defensive and far more open-minded than we've ever been. We're willing and able to reassess our values, assumptions, ideals, goals, and aspirations.

Underlying it all is a gradual but steady rise in self-esteem. We're learning to trust our intuitions and insights, to care about ourselves, and even to love ourselves.

THOUGHT FOR TODAY: Do I know the difference between obsessive awareness of self, and honest self-awareness?

Self-awareness   170

I sometimes think about my attitudes and behavior in the "old days." I'm amazed at how unaware I was of the forces that drove me, the self-deception that kept me going, and the destruction I left in my wake.

Becoming self-aware has been a slow process. Occasionally, however, I've had major insights which, in a relatively short time, have dramatically changed my life.

Several years into recovery, for example, I became aware that I thrived on crisis. When a crisis occurred, I exacerbated it; when a crisis was lacking, I created one. In retrospect, my motivation was to blind myself and those around me to the *real* problems in my life—my alcoholism, my self-centeredness, my emotional immaturity.

Similarly, at one point I became sharply aware that I was largely responsible for my own alienation. Because of my extremely low sense of self-worth, I did everything in my power to keep people away.

In both of these cases, once I saw the causes and effects of my actions, I became willing to seek a new direction. Thankfully, my awarenesses continue to expand and benefit me. When old patterns emerge, I'm able to recognize them and do what's necessary to get back on track.

THOUGHT FOR TODAY: Self-awareness is my springboard to change and growth.

Self-awareness

May 30

We know by now that our reactions to the events in our lives can cause us more grief than the events themselves. We've learned that on "those days," the real problem isn't our boss, our spouse, or the weather, but the way we react to whatever is going on.

We certainly don't want to stop reacting entirely, for our reactions are part of our humanness. In fact, our reactions—be they appropriate or inappropriate—give us continuing opportunities to learn more about ourselves, to steadily increase our self-awareness.

Suppose, for example, we're confronted with an unexpected financial burden and react as if it's the end of the world. This response tells us that we probably need to work on our fear of financial insecurity. Or let's say that we invariably react dramatically to minor adversities. Exploring the underlying causes of such behavior, we may find an immature need for attention, or a tendency toward self-pity.

Our reactions can also show us the progress we're making. When we react with pleasure rather than envy to a friend's good fortune, it's evident that we're becoming less self-centered. And when we turn to God rather than react with panic when facing uncertainty, we're aware of our deepening faith.

THOUGHT FOR TODAY: I can learn a lot about myself from my reactions.

Self-awareness   172

How can we remain self-aware and avoid slipping back to our old ways of self-deception, denial, or outright obliviousness? How can we continue to learn more about ourselves?

One of the surest ways, we have found, is to thoroughly review each day's events, paying special attention to our feelings and behavior. We regularly ask ourselves, for example, if we have any unfinished personal business. Is there something we've kept bottled up, rather than communicated to another person? If so, why?

In order to gain self-awareness, we also try to pinpoint the motives and character traits behind our actions. We try to determine if we've been unfair, unkind, and uncaring—or if we've been honest, helpful, patient, and understanding.

If we find we've been in the wrong, we make amends when they're called for. And if we find that we've been living up to our new goals and values, we give ourselves credit.

If we take these actions on a regular basis—emphasizing self-honesty—more and more will be revealed. We will feel right with ourselves and know exactly where we stand in the world.

THOUGHT FOR TODAY: A self-survey tonight can keep me self-aware and on course.

June 1

Until we made self-assessment a part of our daily routine, we were like travelers without maps. We had a spiritual destination, but weren't at all sure how to move toward it. We didn't know what paths to follow, what areas to avoid, or where to stop and explore.

Through daily reviews of our attitudes and actions, we've gained practical awarenesses; we're now better equipped to make progress in the right direction. We may see that we've developed greater tolerance, for example, but perhaps we need to communicate more openly. Or maybe it has become evident that there are emotional fences to be mended in our relationships.

In many instances, our new awarenesses have provided us with the means and motivation to make beneficial changes. By identifying and seeking solutions for our fears and resentments, we're able to avoid harmful buildups of these and other negative emotions. Similarly, because we take the time to concentrate on problems and do what's necessary to resolve them, our relationships are for the most part free of tension.

Certainly we're a lot more comfortable now that we've learned to spot, acknowledge, and correct our flaws on a daily basis. We have a formula for good living, and a vehicle for spiritual progress.

THOUGHT FOR TODAY: Daily self-assessment shows me where I've been, where I need to go, and how to get there.

Self-awareness   174

Dramatic changes in my life-style, and a circle of trusted new friends—that's what made it possible for me to gain self-awareness during the first years of recovery. I shared and listened openly and honestly; I wrote about my feelings and fears; I attempted to pray and meditate; and I had periodic flashes of insight. Although my progress was gradual, I was nevertheless encouraged by how much I was finding out about myself.

But I eventually learned through experience that self-awareness alone is not enough; it is only *part* of the growth process. Awarenesses, no matter how revealing, can be maximized only when one has the willingness to change, and the courage to take decisive actions.

Early in my sobriety, for example, I was told unequivocally that resentments could be deadly for recovering people. So I did what I could to get rid of my resentments—*all but two of them*. As the result, I remained in a painful limbo, aware of the harm those resentments were causing me, yet unwilling to take the actions that would set me free.

Since that time, I've taken steps to more quickly bridge the gap between awareness and action. I've become adamantly unwilling to pay the price for doing nothing, when I know better.

THOUGHT FOR TODAY: Self-awareness gives me choices. It's up to me to make them.

Self-awareness

June 3

Affirmation

I once was reluctant, even afraid, to gain awarenesses about myself. Today, however, I welcome each new revelation, for I know it has the potential to change my life for the better.

Through a flood of continuing insights in recovery, I've come to know my true self. For the first time I have a solid understanding of my values, capabilities, goals, and aspirations. Now that I know who I am and where I stand in the world, I'm less vulnerable to negative influences that can sidetrack me.

Today I give major priority to expanding my self-awareness. As the result, I have choices beyond anything I could have imagined in the past. I'm no longer confined to a prison of ignorance and closed-mindedness, but am free to learn, to grow, and to move forward emotionally and spiritually.

I am especially grateful for a growing awareness of my personal assets. With the help of God and my fellows, I will try to reverse a lifelong pattern by fully appreciating rather than deprecating those good qualities.

THOUGHT FOR TODAY: I will embrace my new awareness, with gratitude that more is being revealed.

23

Resentment

To be angry about trifles is mean and childish; to rage and be furious is brutish; and to maintain perpetual wrath is akin to the practice and temper of devils; but to prevent and suppress rising resentment is wise and glorious, is manly and divine.

—ISAAC WATTS

June 4

One of the first things we were told in recovery was that resentments are deadly. That was news to us—despite the fact that we had been eaten alive by resentments from grade school into adulthood.

We certainly knew what it felt like to harbor lingering grudges against people and institutions, but we had no clear idea of what resentments actually are. We learned that they are unresolved feelings of hurt, anger, and even hatred—the festering aftermath of real or imagined wrongs against us.

Given that basic understanding, it wasn't hard to zero in on our long-standing resentments: the parents who practically "ruined our lives," the partner who deserted us, the bank that repossessed our car.

More importantly, we began to see just how our resentments harm us—that they are indeed deadly. They keep us in constant emotional jeopardy; we never know when something will ignite our smoldering anger or add fuel to our painful obsessions. When we hold on to resentments it's virtually impossible to live comfortably in the present; we're too busy reliving past hurts and planning future retribution.

Without a doubt, serenity and spiritual comfort will elude us as long as resentments cloud our thinking and upset our priorities.

THOUGHT FOR TODAY: We are the ones who get burned by our smoldering resentments.

Resentment   **178**

When I indulge in anger long enough for a resentment to germinate, it's not very often that I allow it to take root. What helps me is to remember three kernels of common sense that were passed along to me by others.

"When you resent someone, they live rent-free in your head." I probably snapped to attention when I first heard that one, because it was something I had done all of my life. These days I refuse to allow anyone or anything to take over my thoughts in that manner. The very idea is intolerable.

"Other people don't even know it when you resent them." It's easy to see the absurdity of my resentment when I picture my "adversary" conducting business as usual while I'm completely distracted—or fast asleep while I'm wide awake.

"The worst thing about resentments is the endless rehearsal of the acts of retribution." I related to that one completely—and still do. How often in the past I had tormented myself, devising elaborate strategies to get even with someone for what he or she had done!

THOUGHT FOR TODAY: In my "new house" there is no room for resentment.

Resentment

June 6

When we put our resentments down in black and white, that's when they started to lose their power. We began by searching our memories and drawing up a "grudge list." It was surprising how many resentments we had, and how long we had been carrying them around!

We looked carefully at each resentment to determine its cause, the way it injured us, and where we might have been to blame. For example, we wrote: "I resent my brother. He mistreated me. This humiliated me and affected my self-esteem. But I often provoked him."

By listing our resentments in this fashion, it became quickly apparent how pointless they were, how they drained us, and how they hampered our spiritual growth. Furthermore, by focusing on our own behavior instead of the wrongs of others, we were able to pinpoint many of our character defects. We were able to see, for example, how often we had acted out of self-centeredness, dishonesty, and fear.

Many of our resentments simply disappeared when we brought them out into the open and looked at them honestly. Others stood out sharply and caused us renewed pain. In those cases the message was clear—still more action was needed if we were to live freely.

THOUGHT FOR TODAY: Many of my resentments will fade away if I put them on paper and admit my role.

Resentment   **180**

There was just so much we could do on our own to get rid of deeply held resentments. We came to believe, through personal experience, that we needed God's help to release us from their grip.

Once we cleared the way by learning all we could through an inventory of our resentments, we had to be sure we were completely willing to have God remove them. We may have been keenly aware of the pain and problems caused by our resentments, but perhaps we were hanging on to them because of hidden payoffs such as self-pity.

When we were ready to let go without reservation, we humbly asked God to remove our resentments. We did so in faith, for we knew that He alone has all power.

In order to further show our willingness, it was suggested that we add another dimension to our spiritual efforts. "Pray for those you resent," we were told. "Ask God to bless them with all the comfort and happiness you wish for yourself."

Our first thought was, "Are you serious?" But when we later followed the advice, admittedly with only partial sincerity, our resentments were indeed lifted. God did for us what we could not do for ourselves.

THOUGHT FOR TODAY: I will do all I can, then I will ask God to do all He can.

June 8

Long after most of my major resentments had been healed, one continued to devour me. It seemed that I would forever bitterly resent my parents for the verbal and emotional abuse they had heaped on me until their last days.

There was no question that the resentment was dragging me backwards. There was no question that it was poisoning me and my view of the world. And there was no question that I had to pull out all the stops in my search for resolution.

Once again I withdrew from the battle. I surrendered and turned my full attention to God. I redoubled my efforts at prayer and meditation, again beseeching Him to remove the resentment.

One day during my meditation it came to me that although I had prayed for my parents, I had never actually forgiven them. I knew then that forgiveness was the answer for me. In time, with God's help, I was able to forgive my parents for their wrongs—and to forgive myself as well.

I suspect that this resentment will never die completely. When I feel it stirring on occasion, I squelch it by immediately turning my thoughts to God—and forgiveness.

THOUGHT FOR TODAY: Resentments can be overcome—with forgiveness and God's help.

Today we're working not only to get rid of the resentments of the past, but also to prevent new ones from developing. We simply can't afford resentments of any kind in our new lives.

But things do happen, and it's pretty difficult to see an upsetting incident as an opportunity for spiritual growth. If we're wronged, we can't pretend that nothing happened, or that we're not angry as a result.

Nevertheless, we're determined to avoid slipping into the emotional quicksand such incidents represent. So when they occur we do everything we can to quiet the disturbance within us—regardless of where it came from or how it got started. Our priority is to keep our hurt feelings from turning into resentment.

It can be helpful to view the wrongdoer's actions with some degree of understanding and tolerance. Perhaps he or she is emotionally or spiritually off balance in some way. From that standpoint, we can ask God to help us feel compassion and empathy for the person, and possibly even show it in some way.

THOUGHT FOR TODAY: The price I paid for past resentments was high enough. I can ill afford any new ones.

June 10

Affirmation

Today I affirm that resentment is the antithesis of spiritual growth. In order to better seek and do God's will, I strive to release past resentments and build harmonious relationships in all areas.

When unresolved feelings of hurt and anger resurface, I will affirm that they are self-defeating and that they distance me from God. I will ask myself: Was I to blame in some way for the original provocation or hurt? Am I unwilling to let go of my resentments for any reason? I will then ask God to release me from them.

When an affront or injury sets my emotions awry, I will concentrate first on calming the disturbance within me. I will resolve potentially harmful situations as they arise, and I will not allow negative feelings to develop into new resentments.

While I can never attain the perfect objective of a resentment-free life, the spiritual principles I have learned will serve me well and bring me ever closer. Surely ill feelings will quickly subside if I practice patience, understanding, compassion, and forgiveness in all my affairs.

THOUGHT FOR TODAY: Resentments hamper my spiritual progress by blocking the channel to God.

24

Willingness to Change

Today is not yesterday. We ourselves change. How then, can our works and thoughts, if they are always to be the fittest, continue always the same? Change, indeed, is painful, yet ever needful; and if memory has its force and worth, so also has hope.

—THOMAS CARLYLE

June 11

In all of our lives there are times when we need and want to change in important ways. Perhaps we're fed up with a lifelong pattern of negative convictions about ourselves. Along with that, we may realize it's necessary to change long-standing attitudes and be-havior patterns, especially those affecting the way we get along with others.

But often, needing and wanting to change is only part of what it takes to do so. More than anything, we must first have genuine willingness to change. How does this come about? How does a person become willing?

Sometimes, simply becoming aware of a harmful reality can automatically bring about the willingness to change. In other instances it may take prolonged pain and suffering to bring us to that point.

Willingness occasionally seems to come out of nowhere. God may grace us with a flash of insight or a moment of clarity, and in the process we become transformed.

In one of its most satisfying manifestations, the willingness to change is a direct outgrowth of the way we value ourselves. As our self-esteem rises—as we begin to feel more deserving of good—we're willing to do what is necessary to allow it into our lives.

THOUGHT FOR TODAY: Have I become convinced that willingness is a prerequisite for change?

Willingness to Change   **186**

"I knew it was time to change, but I just wasn't willing," a friend said. "The biggest stumbling block, I think, was being afraid to reach out and ask for help. The idea of getting involved with other people at such a personal level really terrified me."

We were talking about the fear of change, and how it had delayed our recoveries. "The same with me," I told my friend. "When I was just a breath away from picking up the phone, the things that stopped me were my shame and my pride. I was afraid to admit how really messed up I was."

One of our biggest fears, we agreed, was facing a disruption in living patterns which, although painful and even life-threatening, were at least familiar and predictable.

"The changes ahead of me were major, I knew that," my friend added. "I also knew they would take a lot of responsibility and action on my part—and I was just plain scared to make that kind of commitment."

"Right," I remembered. "And also scared to take the risk, to make a mistake—to *fail*."

THOUGHT FOR TODAY: If I am fearful when facing change, I will do my footwork and trust God to do the rest.

June 13

Why is willingness so hard to come by at certain times? Why do we dig our heels into the status quo even when we know it's time to change? There can be several reasons, and not always obvious ones.

It's possible, among other things, that we're getting hidden payoffs from the behavior we'd like to change. Let's say we've become aware that our tendency to be manipulative and controlling is causing problems in our relationships. But the payoff is that we often get our own way—and we *like* that.

If we are adult children of alcoholics or have similarly dysfunctional backgrounds, our unwillingness to make a change for the better may flow directly from low self-esteem. Without realizing it, we may feel that we deserve the misery or unsatisfactory conditions of our life.

Moreover, because of our backgrounds we may feel that we are entitled to certain character defects—such as self-pity and anger—as "recompense" for our suffering in the past.

If we are having difficulty developing the willingness to change, perhaps it's time to search for the hidden reasons behind our reluctance. By doing so, it's likely we'll soon be well on our way to taking that all-important first step toward change.

THOUGHT FOR TODAY: Smooth the way toward change by digging out and clearing away any hidden obstacles.

I can still see myself slumped forward at the bar, torn apart inside, knowing how much I was hurting the people who loved me. They kept pressuring me to stop drinking, but I continued to do so for several more years.

I couldn't be forced; the willingness to change had to come from within. It was only then that sobriety would become possible.

Since that time I have developed other firm beliefs about willingness. For one thing, it's not necessary to acquire complete willingness all at once. Even a small amount can be the key that unlocks the door to change. Once the door is slightly ajar, it can be opened wider and wider.

I've become convinced, in addition, that in my life there is a dynamic link between my willingness to change and my receptivity to God's power in helping bring it about. In other words, if I show God through my footwork that I am willing to change, He always provides for me.

I recall reading that change is invariably an *exchange*. In recovery I am exchanging a way of life that brought only anguish and discord, for one centered around spiritual principles and the possibility of limitless freedom and peace of mind.

THOUGHT FOR TODAY: Willingness is the key that can open the door to change and a better life.

June 15

You want to make a change, desperately so, almost to the point of obsession. You've done everything you can think of to become willing . . . .

You've rehashed your circumstances over and over, and you fully acknowledge the necessity for change. You've dwelled at length on the good things in store when you finally make a start. You've mapped a detailed course of action, and have gone so far as to catalog the fears that are holding you back. You've done it all, it seems, but you still haven't been able to clear the hurdle of unwillingness.

It suddenly occurs to you then that you don't have to do it alone. You can rely on faith and turn to God to help you bring about what you haven't been able to achieve on your own.

How you communicate with God is of course unique to you alone, but in essence you ask Him to grant the willingness to be willing. In your prayers you ask for freedom from the fears, stubbornness, or lingering doubts that are holding you back. You pray for the courage to move forward.

The results are not necessarily apparent overnight, or even in weeks. But you keep praying, for from past experience you are well aware of the rewards of faith.

THOUGHT FOR TODAY: Pray for the willingness to be willing.

Willingness to Change 190

I once found the fossilized shell of a giant mollusk while I was walking through the hills near my home. When I glance at the fossil these days, I try to imagine what the local landscape was like when it was below sea level thousands of years ago. I think about the inevitability and constancy of change.

There was a time in my life when I saw change as solely a negative force. It was difficult for me to accept change of any kind, and I put a lot of effort and energy into keeping things the same. Needless to say, it was a losing battle.

Over time I've developed quite a different attitude. I've come to believe that change is usually beneficial and frequently exciting, not only as it alters the world around us, but as it affects me personally.

When I find myself resisting change, I try to remember that God is the creator and regulator of all that takes place in my life. I remind myself that no matter what occurs, His plan for good will prevail.

THOUGHT FOR TODAY: I will try to see change as an expression of God's grace. I will try to accept change gracefully.

Willingness to Change

June 17

Affirmation

Change is a vitalizing force in my life. I welcome and embrace change, for without it there can be no growth, no progress, no spirit of joy.

I have faith that God's wisdom and purpose underlies all change. Although I may not fully understand why a particular change is occurring at a particular time, I will try to see it as an integral part of God's plan for ultimate good. If on occasion I am temporarily overwhelmed by the magnitude of change in my life, I will remember that *change is always an exchange*, and that God never gives me more than I can handle.

Experience has taught me that willingness is the key to inner change; even a small amount can open the door. From that point on, my willingness can grow, opening the door ever wider.

In the past, my unwillingness to change caused stagnation and regression. Today, in contrast, rising self-esteem motivates me to take actions that further my progress. I am grateful for this new attitude. I am grateful that I now feel deserving of the beneficial changes resulting from my willingness and God's grace.

THOUGHT FOR TODAY: Without change there can be no recovery; without willingness there can be no change.

Willingness to Change   192

25

Expectations

I can pardon everybody's mistakes except my own.
—MARCUS CATO THE ELDER

June 18

"That's not good enough, you're hopeless." "It's your own fault, you're not trying hard enough." "You'll never do it right!"

When we remember the way we were ridiculed or punished because we didn't meet our parents' expectations of us, it's easy to see why in later years we found it almost impossible to approve of ourselves. The messages we received as children became our own messages. No matter how hard we tried or how well we performed, it was never good enough.

By riding ourselves so relentlessly, some of us went far in our careers. But even then we couldn't enjoy our success, because we could never be satisfied with what we had accomplished. Our expectations of ourselves were insatiable and completely unattainable.

Obviously there's not much room for happiness or self-esteem in that sort of a life. That's why, in recovery, we're giving high priority to overcoming those die-hard admonitions of yesterday. That's why we're putting our past and present in perspective and asking some long-overdue questions: Are people all wrong when they compliment us or take note of our accomplishments today? Haven't we made remarkable progress, considering where we came from? Isn't it time to get off our own backs and to start feeling good about ourselves?

THOUGHT FOR TODAY: The best I can do *is* good enough.

Expectations   194

My car wouldn't go into gear one day, so I slid underneath to see if I could spot the trouble. I had absolutely no idea what I was doing when I jerked a lever alongside the transmission. The car went into neutral and rolled backwards, pinning my shoulder under a wheel. No bones were broken, but I was badly bruised and extremely sore.

What was even worse was the way I castigated myself for making such a dumb mistake. For almost a week I punished myself mercilessly, until a friend set me straight. "Enough already," he pleaded. "You made a mistake, you're human. So forgive yourself and let it go."

Later on I thought back to the days when self-reproach was a way of life for me, when every mistake that I made, no matter how small or insignificant, was unforgivable. It was difficult to believe that I once had such perennially unrealistic expectations—that I was so hard on myself for so long.

Thank God I'm more accepting of myself today—of my limitations as well as my capabilities. Thank God I can learn from my mistakes most of the time, without judging myself harshly.

THOUGHT FOR TODAY: If I make a mistake I will try to be patient rather than punitive with myself.

June 20

It's impossible to achieve perfection—we all know that. Yet many of us still expect ourselves to have perfect skills, perfect behavior, and even perfect thoughts. We try to be perfect parents, perfect employees, perfect friends. Needless to say our fruitless pursuit leaves us feeling frustrated and disappointed in ourselves.

Why do we persist? Low self-esteem usually has a lot to do with it. We may reason, "If I'm perfect I'll prove my value—and then you'll like me." Or perhaps we feel, deep down, that we deserve to fail; our blind quest for perfection sets us up to do just that time and time again.

As our self-esteem rises in recovery, our need for perfection diminishes. We realize that most of the people in our lives accept us as we are—and we're beginning to accept ourselves in the same way.

Today we strive for progress rather than perfection. This is true not only for personal goals, but spiritual ones as well. We take great comfort in our conviction that only God is infallible. He wants us to be happy, joyous, and free—not perfect.

THOUGHT FOR TODAY: When I start to make unreasonable demands of myself, I will remember that my goal is progress, not perfection.

Expectations   196

We were talking about living at one extreme or the other, with no middle ground, when my friend remembered her first job during recovery as a tree nursery manager. "Even though sales improved—and the crew's work habits did too—I never felt I was doing a good enough job. That's how insecure I was," she said. "It had nothing to do with the owners. They made it clear they were pleased with me.

"I put more and more pressure on myself, and kept taking responsibility that wasn't even mine, without realizing it. I drove myself nuts. The quality of my life just deteriorated.

"You can guess what happened next," my friend continued. "I went to the other extreme and completely gave up. Since I had made my job impossible in my mind, I decided it *was* impossible. I was ready to quit."

"Did you?" I asked.

"Fortunately no," she said. "I talked to somebody first—a good friend—and she pointed out that the problem had absolutely nothing to do with the job, and everything to do with my outlandish expectations of myself. It was a good lesson. I still push myself, but not so hard and not to the edge."

THOUGHT FOR TODAY: Where is the pressure coming from? Is it real—or am I generating it?

June 22

For years we rose and fell in accordance with whether or not our expectations were met. Most of the time we fell. We were frequently frustrated and upset because it seemed that people and institutions had let us down.

We entered relationships with preconceived ideas of what we would get from our partner, and of what he or she needed from us. We anticipated that our parents would shower us with approval for our achievements. We counted on receiving a bonus for completing a project at work. Over and over we were disappointed. We felt constantly betrayed.

As we've become less self-centered, our view of the world—and our relationship to it—has changed. We see now that our pain wasn't really caused by others and life, but by what we expected from others and life. We finally figured out that people don't exist to satisfy our needs, and that it's not their written-in-stone obligation to come through for us.

More and more we're able to simply let things happen—to accept life on life's terms. It's so much easier and so much more comfortable living this way.

THOUGHT FOR TODAY: Reduced expectations equal reduced disappointment, frustration, and pain.

Where did my overblown expectations of myself and others lead? They led to failure after failure, or at least the pervasive sense of failure. When I entered recovery, the unfulfilled expectations in my life loomed so large that I saw *myself* as a complete failure.

Although I had in fact frequently let myself and others down in the past, I now realize that my failures weren't always what they appeared to be. I often "failed" to achieve goals simply because I had set them way beyond my capabilities. I had "failed" because I expected perfection in all areas. I had "failed" if in my own eyes I had somehow been inadequate, or had done something to be ashamed of.

Over time my beliefs about failure have changed dramatically in other ways as well. I have learned through experience that a seeming failure often turns out to be a necessary stepping-stone toward spiritual growth.

These days when I "fail" to achieve a goal or to fulfill an expectation, I try to consider the outcome in this context: Perhaps it wasn't meant to be; perhaps it's not part of God's plan for me right now.

THOUGHT FOR TODAY: Have I failed? Or have I failed to see what God wants me to see?

Affirmation

I take great comfort in the knowledge that I am a spiritual being. God has a plan of good for me, and I can rely on Him to lead me forward on paths of freedom, happiness, and well-being.

This awareness helps me release the burden of my unrealistic expectations. It allows me to accept myself as I am, my limitations as well as my capabilities. It allows me to accept others as they are and choose to be. It allows me to accept life as it unfolds.

Today I will not expect myself to know all, do all, and be all. I will abandon each and every expectation that has the potential to cause disappointment and pain, that supports the idea that life is an unending struggle.

Today I will ask God to free me from my tormenting need to be perfect. I will try to learn from my mistakes, and to see my seeming failures as stepping stones along the pathway of spiritual growth. I will strive for progress, not perfection.

THOUGHT FOR TODAY: God is in charge. I will abandon my self-defeating objectives and let Him take me on to better things.

26

Acceptance

Affliction comes to us all not to make us sad, but sober; not to make us sorry, but wise; not to make us despondent, but by its darkness to refresh us, as the night refreshes the day; not to impoverish, but to enrich us, as the plough enriches the field; to multiply our joy, as the seed by planting is multiplied a thousand-fold.

—HENRY WARD BEECHER

June 25

I used to put myself through the wringer when challenged by unexpected or seemingly negative events. My overflowing anger kept me off balance for days and sometimes weeks. I complained bitterly and all but drowned in self-pity. Even when I faced minor upsets or disappointments I frequently fell apart.

Today it's a different story. I try to concentrate my energies into accepting things as they are, rather than wishing they were different. For I have seen in my own life and the lives of many others that acceptance is the surest way to peace of mind.

By no means have I come anywhere near complete success in changing my responses to unforeseen situations. For the most part, however, I am conscientious in my efforts to practice acceptance, and I continue to make progress.

When I "go with the flow," I tend to be more flexible and open-minded, and it's easier for me to adapt to changing circumstances. I'm also less likely to become distracted and anxious. When I focus on acceptance, everyday problems diminish in size rather than grow larger than life. Serenity is then within my grasp.

THOUGHT FOR TODAY: I will find peace of mind by practicing acceptance.

The locations alone are depressingly familiar—a hospital waiting room, a lawyer's office, an empty house. Most of us have experienced the feelings of frustration and helplessness that can arise in such settings.

No matter what the particulars during these times of crisis, the spiritual principle of acceptance can quiet the inner turmoil and help us transcend our difficulties. As helpless as we may feel in most respects, there are always steps we can take to become more accepting.

Initially, we can try to regain objectivity by figuratively stepping away, mentally and emotionally. We are then better able to "reperceive" the situation without being influenced by fear, denial, or other people's involvement.

We can try to determine what actions, if any, should be taken to help ourselves and others. At the same time, we can do our best to come to terms with our powerlessness.

Because God is an ever-reliable source of guidance and strength in all matters, we can gain the greatest acceptance by placing the problem in His hands. We can remind ourselves that He has an important reason for every occurrence and circumstance, even though it may be beyond our own understanding.

THOUGHT FOR TODAY: Even if there's nothing we can do, there's always *one* thing we can do: Strive for acceptance.

June 27

A group of friends and I were sitting in a coffee shop. When the subject of acceptance came up, one of the men began to talk about a problem he had just begun to overcome. "I almost lost my job because I was coming in late every day," he told us. "I was behind in my rent, and I hadn't made out a tax return in four years.

"My life was a shambles because of my irresponsibility. That was the first thing I had to accept. The next thing I had to accept was the seriousness of my problem—and that it would just keep getting worse unless I did something about it."

He noted that he wasn't at all irresponsible during his youth. In fact, his drug-addicted parents relied on him to handle responsibilities ranging from marketing and cleaning to occasionally raising bail.

"I really resented all that responsibility back then," he said. "And maybe that explains my *irre*sponsibility as an adult.

"The hardest thing to accept is the solution," he concluded. "You know, getting help, learning how to change my habit patterns, putting yesterday behind me."

THOUGHT FOR TODAY: Now that I accept the problem and its cause, am I willing to accept the solution?

Relationships were never our strong suit. To this day many of us have difficulty getting along with neighbors, relatives, and especially those we live and work with. The heart of the problem is our inability or unwillingness to accept others as they are.

In various ways, including sarcasm, manipulation, or out-and-out threats, we try to make the people in our lives change to suit us. We pressure partners to embrace spirituality as we have. We lecture coworkers about their job performance. We criticize friends for their political views. What happens, invariably, is that we cause tension and disharmony in our relationships and end up even more frustrated than before.

We are learning that acceptance is an essential ingredient in successful relationships. The way we practice acceptance, purely and simply, is by allowing others the personal freedom to live according to their own choices, no matter how we may feel about it. It's not only that we have no business trying to change other people's beliefs and behavior, but that we are in fact powerless to do so.

THOUGHT FOR TODAY: My relationships will improve if I focus on my own shortcomings and accept other people as they are.

Acceptance

June 29

Recently we have been berating ourselves for not making more rapid progress in recovery. Perhaps a character defect we thought was behind us has resurfaced, and once again we're disgusted with ourselves. Or maybe we haven't been able to quiet the buzz of fear accompanying our interactions with other people—and that continues to frustrate and anger us. In short, we're having trouble accepting ourselves as we are, our weaknesses along with our strengths.

We know that it's easier to move forward from a starting point of self-acceptance than from one of self-hatred. Yet that knowledge doesn't seem to be enough; we're still too harsh and impatient with ourselves.

At times like these, many of us find solace and support by turning to God. We reflect on the certainty that He accepts us exactly as we are. We focus on His unconditional love, reassuring ourselves that He does not withhold acceptance until we have become free of our character defects, or we have reached specific spiritual "milestones." In our prayers, we ask for God's help in accepting ourselves as He does.

THOUGHT FOR TODAY: God accepts me as I am.

Every so often it occurs to me that I truly wouldn't want to trade places with anyone else in the world. With a deep sense of gratitude, I suddenly realize that I'm *okay* with who I am.

The feeling has nothing to do with physical appearance, occupation, or who my friends are. It has everything to do with finally accepting myself from the inside out, and beginning to care about the real me. This is a very special kind of transformation; it looms almost as large as the miracle of my sobriety.

I had always wished to be somebody else. I yearned to be more self-assured, more likeable, more respectable, more articulate, more at ease among people. I spent most of my life comparing my insides to other people's outsides.

It took years for the transformation to evolve. It didn't come about because I saw myself as finally "measuring up"; it wasn't that I had at long last acquired those qualities I envied in others. All of those things had become irrelevant. The release from self-abnegation came through a gradual acceptance of myself—the person I once was, the person I am, the person I am becoming.

THOUGHT FOR TODAY: Self-acceptance is a very special miracle, a very special freedom.

Acceptance

July 1

Affirmation

Acceptance is the way to peace of mind. No matter where I am or what I am going through, I can reduce stress, gain inner calm, and live more harmoniously with my fellows by applying this fundamental spiritual principle.

I need not wait for calamities to occur before I seek acceptance. The principle offers me a simple and sure remedy for any of the frustrations and minor upsets I face on a daily basis.

Where I once believed that acceptance could be practiced only by "spiritually enlightened" people, I now realize that its rewards are available to anyone. In fact, as I have learned, it is the very practice of acceptance that can further one's overall spiritual progress.

I find, for example, that my relationships are healthier when I try to accept others as they are, rather than wish they were different. Practicing acceptance in this manner—along with its concomitants of tolerance, patience, and understanding—helps me to become less self-centered and gain humility.

In the same way, my continuing goal is to become more *self*-accepting. One day at a time, I am striving to accept myself in the same unconditional way that God accepts me.

THOUGHT FOR TODAY: By practicing acceptance, I also practice such other spiritual principles as tolerance, understanding, and forgiveness.

27

Gratitude

We can be thankful to a friend for a few acres or a little money; and yet for the freedom and command of the whole earth, and for the great benefits of our being, our life, health, and reason, we look upon ourselves as under no obligation.

—SENECA

July 2

Gratitude bubbles through us like adrenaline when something good comes our way. There is a "rush"—we all know what it feels like—when we receive a windfall, when we get exciting news, or when an unexpected bonus falls into our lap.

We feel warm and confident inside. We feel elated and special. We find ourselves thinking about God, and appreciating what He has done for us.

But, needless to say, incidents of extraordinary good fortune are usually few and far between. That being the case, most of us don't experience feelings of gratitude very often. And as the result, we miss out on the unique sense of well-being that it brings.

The thing is, we can feel grateful anytime we choose—we don't have to wait for a bonanza. We can consciously cultivate an "attitude of gratitude" any time of the day, any day of the week. Our blessings and good fortune may not be along material lines, or even tangible, but heaven knows each of us has much to be thankful for. Just think about it for a minute . . . .

THOUGHT FOR TODAY: Have I thought about my blessings today? Have I made a mental (or written) list of the things I have to be grateful for?

More and more these days, I experience moments and even hours of happiness, peace of mind, and the feeling that I am right with myself and the world.

At such times, I am profoundly grateful not only for my recovery and what has subsequently taken place in my life, but also for the anguish and fear that brought me to the point of surrender. For I truly believe that it was necessary for me to endure the pain of yesterday in order to receive and appreciate the blessings of today.

I am grateful for God's presence, and for the spiritual tools that have enabled me to regain my health and begin to live again.

I am grateful that I have learned to understand, accept, and forgive those who harmed me in the past—and to forgive myself for similar wrongs.

I am grateful to be free of the rage and resentment I carried around for so long.

I am grateful to have progressed from alienation and loneliness to fellowship and a sense of belonging.

I am grateful for the privilege of helping others by sharing my own experience, strength, and hope.

THOUGHT FOR TODAY: Everything I went through in the past made me what I am today. I have no regrets, only gratitude.

July 4

We may not want to admit it, but sometimes it doesn't take much to throw us off balance and make us feel sorry for ourselves. A week-long siege of the flu, too much overtime, bad weather—we can each create our own list of misfortunes.

For many of us, the "poor me" syndrome is like a comfortable chair; we can slip back into it without even thinking. When we do, our attitude soon begins to contaminate everything in and around us. At that point, it often seems difficult to get up again.

The solution, of course, is to recognize all we have to be grateful for. True, we've heard that a hundred times, but it always bears repeating.

This is not to suggest that we be grateful for working late or for having the flu. But if we think back to the way we used to be—if we think about people with no jobs, and far more serious illnesses—it's a lot easier to accept our "high-class" problems as the relatively minor annoyances that they are. And once we do that, we can be grateful for who we are, what we have, and where we are headed.

THOUGHT FOR TODAY: Gratitude helps me keep it in perspective.

People who knew us as we were sometimes say, "You've done so well!" When we hear those words, we may be tempted to congratulate ourselves and take credit for the abundance in our lives. But we are reminded, instead, that everything we have is a gift from God.

God has shown us that our needs will always be met, in the best manner and at the right time. Knowing that He cares for us in this way gives us a solid sense of inner security. And we are deeply grateful.

The more we rely on God, the less we are tyrannized by our fears and doubts. Whenever we are uncertain of what path to take, or what choice to make, we know we can turn to Him for guidance and strength. And we are deeply grateful.

God has made it possible for us to experience and freely participate in the wondrous world that He has created. He has given each of us special talents and capabilities with which we can bring joy and enrichment not only to our own lives, but also the lives of others. And we are deeply grateful.

THOUGHT FOR TODAY: Everything I have, and everything I am becoming—these are gifts from God.

July 6

It's difficult now to pinpoint the actual dates, places, or circumstances, but there were times in our lives when we would have given all we had for things to be different.

We cried out to be freed of pain. We pleaded for help. We prayed to be taken from where we were to a better place. And here we are. We have been given this day, this new day. It is brimming with promise.

Where it once took all our energy just to get through the day, we now have the opportunity to discover more about ourselves and the world around us.

Instead of hiding or numbing our feelings, as we did in the past, we can fine-tune our senses and participate fully in the day as it unfolds.

Where we used to live in fear and isolation, today we have the chance to live in fellowship and harmony with others. We can enhance our own experiences by sharing them with friends.

We have been given this day, and it is ours to live as we choose. By pausing now and then to give thanks, we can savor our feelings of gratitude.

THOUGHT FOR TODAY: If I remain open-minded and aware, today's opportunities will be boundless.

My brother once purchased a watch with several unique features, including a mechanical sun which "rose" during the day, and a moon which appeared at night. Had such a timepiece been available during my drinking years, I would have bought it without hesitation.

When I was on a binge, I invariably blacked out. I lost track not only of where I had been and what I had done, but also of time itself—mornings, afternoons, evenings, entire days. I never admitted it to anyone, but sometimes I would wake up and have no idea whether it was dawn or dusk.

There would be soft, gray light coming through a window. The hands on my watch would tell me that it was five or six o'clock, but I couldn't tell whether it was the beginning or end of the day. I wouldn't know whether to get dressed for work, or to get ready for dinner. So I would just lie there, peering into the grayness, paralyzed with terror.

Every time I see my brother's watch, with its funny little sun and moon, I'm instantly transported back to those moments. And I'm overwhelmed with gratitude that I've been restored to sobriety and sanity.

THOUGHT FOR TODAY: Remembering the past, even briefly, will keep me from taking the present for granted.

July 8

Affirmation

I am grateful, God, for my new life. Because of your loving kindness, I have regained my self-esteem and have become capable of giving and receiving love. I am now a productive and whole person, part of the solution rather than the problem.

I am grateful, God, that you have created a perfect plan for my destiny. You have led me unerringly through the dark days of the past to the brightness and joy of the present. It is deeply comforting to know that I can always turn to you for guidance, courage, and strength.

I am grateful, God, for all you have given me, and for all you have taken away. Thank you for soundness of mind, the will to live, and the desire to continue growing along spiritual lines. Thank you for relieving me of the bondage of self, and for taking away my obsessions and character flaws.

I am grateful, God, that my faith in you allows me to live without fear. Thank you for self-confidence and a sense of well-being. And thank you, dear God, for making it possible for me to feel this way right now.

THOUGHT FOR TODAY: Thanks to God, I am faith-filled, fearless, and free.

28

Responsibility

People think responsibility is hard to bear. It's not. I think that sometimes it is the absence of responsibility that is harder to bear. You have a great feeling of impotence.

—HENRY KISSINGER

July 9

Every so often something reminds us sharply of how irresponsible we used to be. We spot a large stack of unopened bills on a neighbor's windowsill. A friend with a toothache confides that he hasn't been to a dentist in years. A coworker is stranded on the freeway because she never bothered to replace the temporary spare after her last flat tire.

Those of us who were irresponsible didn't make a conscious decision to be that way, but neither did the behavioral pattern develop by accident. In some cases we became irresponsible adults because we lacked guidance as children; our role models never taught us or showed us how to be responsible.

Very often, fear ruled our lives—to the extent that we couldn't deal with real problems in a real world. Even when we knew that it was absolutely necessary to take care of something, our paralyzing fear prevented us from accepting the responsibility.

But no matter what caused our irresponsibility, we all decided to do something about it for the same reason. Our lives had become unmanageable, and we simply weren't willing to live like that anymore.

THOUGHT FOR TODAY: I choose to be responsible. I choose to live life on life's terms.

Taking care of responsibilities was hardly a top priority in my old life. I was usually just one step ahead of disaster, always playing catch-up. *Survival* was my priority. Needless to say, I didn't have a high opinion of myself.

Building self-esteem has been an ongoing process, and thankfully I've made considerable progress over time. As for dramatic impact in that area, probably nothing will ever match my first successes in taking responsibility.

I can still remember how good it made me feel when I was able to balance my checkbook without needing to hide evidences of financial irresponsibility. How proud I was when I could finally "be there" for a friend or family member who needed help. What a boost to my self-worth when I started taking responsibility for my health after years of neglect and abuse.

It even seemed miraculous when I began doing what most people take for granted: showing up somewhere when I said I would; keeping a promise; meeting a deadline.

In truth, it still makes me feel good in those same ways when I am responsible. I thank God that my life has changed and my priorities have shifted.

THOUGHT FOR TODAY: Now that I have become responsible, I have a far better opinion of myself.

Responsibility

July 11

Anyone who has ever been involved with a chemically or behaviorally dependent parent, spouse, sibling, child, or friend knows how we suffer when we assume responsibility for another person's life. We become victims of alcoholism or gambling without ever touching a drop or placing a bet; we become victims of other people's obsessions and compulsions without ever actually participating in their activities.

We are victimized not so much by our loved ones' disorders as we are by our own feelings and reactions. We make *ourselves* sick trying to control someone else's choices, actions, emotions, and destiny. We center our lives around trying to anticipate, solve, or cover up other people's problems. And when our help is rejected or is ineffective, we feel self-pity, guilt, frustration, and anger.

Our recovery from codependency can begin only when we realize we are truly powerless over the thoughts, attitudes, and actions of others. That is the reality. Only when we accept it and detach ourselves can we become free. Only when we learn to "let go and let God" can we live our own lives.

THOUGHT FOR TODAY: Have I become convinced that my first responsibility is my own recovery?

It has been years since you moved out of your parents' home, yet you're still struggling to shed the cloak of responsibility you took upon yourself growing up.

When your mother or father got drunk or abusive, you wondered what you had done to set them off. When they fought about money, infidelity, or anything else—even when they were depressed or irritable—you knew it was somehow your fault. If they separated or divorced, you felt completely responsible.

The circumstances of your life are entirely different these days, but you still feel responsible for everything that goes on around you. You put tremendous pressure on yourself to make sure your companion or date is having a good time. You assume full responsibility and criticize yourself mercilessly when something goes wrong at work. In short, the responsibility you take upon yourself is still out of sync with reality—and it's making you miserable.

It's time to give yourself a break. When you start to take on responsibility that isn't yours, try to see how you're hurting yourself. Remember that your goal is self-affirmation, not self-deprecation. Remind yourself that lack of power is not your weakness, but your strength.

THOUGHT FOR TODAY: Am I still using misplaced responsibility as a way to attack myself?

Responsibility

July 13

Recovery often requires major changes in the ways we perceive and deal with responsibility. We may have to redefine responsibility, before determining how it best fits into our new life. We may have to work toward achieving a new balance—between taking on responsibility that is rightfully ours, and letting go of responsibility that doesn't belong to us.

Even while we're successfully meeting these challenges, we sometimes can be thrown off by someone who tries to manage and control our every move. A parent, true to form, tries to influence each decision we make. A friend inundates us with unsolicited advice and fully expects us to take it. A spouse withholds approval unless we do things his or her way.

When we're faced with these kinds of intrusions, it may be necessary to establish boundaries and stand our ground. Once we decide what we can put up with and what we can't, it's probably a good idea to talk frankly yet tolerantly with the person involved.

We may be successful in gaining the person's understanding, or we may not. Whatever the case, we need to continue to make our own decisions, to be our own person, to be responsible.

THOUGHT FOR TODAY: When I state my case, I am taking responsibility for myself.

There's no question in my mind that my recovery from alcoholism, and the miraculous changes in my life, are due to the presence and power of God. He has made possible what previously was impossible, and I have faith that He will continue to do so.

There's also no question that my recovery will continue only as long as I take the responsibility that is mine. I can't sit back and expect God to do it all.

Certainly I have to continue taking responsibility for my own actions. I'm the only one who can decide whether or not to pick up the first drink, or to be honest in all I say or do. Only I can choose to practice spiritual principles as I interact with others each day.

I also believe that it's my responsibility to pass on what I have learned by sharing feelings, experiences, and ideas with other recovering people.

My personal responsibilities include strengthening my inner self. I try to accomplish this by seeking new awarenesses, by letting go of character defects, and by striving to enhance my relationship with God through prayer and meditation.

THOUGHT FOR TODAY: Am I fully participating in my own recovery?

July 15

Affirmation

There's a new balance to the way I approach responsibility, in contrast to yesterday's all-or-nothing extremes. Today I know where my responsibilities lie; I know when to take action, when to draw back, and when to let go and accept my powerlessness.

I'm grateful that I no longer feel compelled to take responsibility for other people's emotions, decisions, misadventures, and ultimate fate.

I'm grateful too that I've learned to be responsible for myself; that I'm endeavoring to fulfill my physical, emotional, and financial needs; that so many changes have come about because of my new approach and actions.

My willingness to be responsible has had a strong, positive impact on my self-esteem. The more footwork I undertake to further my progress, the better I feel about myself.

There's a new order and solidity to my life now that I'm fully functional and able to take care of my commitments on a daily basis. I've come to grips with responsibility in affirmative and constructive ways, and as a result I'm gaining self-respect as well as the respect of others.

THOUGHT FOR TODAY: I'm grateful that I've become responsible in ways that count: for *my* actions, *my* choices, *my* happiness, *my* well-being.

29

Coming to Terms with the Past

Nor deem the irrevocable past as wholly wasted, wholly vain, if rising on its wrecks, at last to something nobler we attain.

—HENRY WADSWORTH LONGFELLOW

July 16

To a large degree, the unresolved issues of the past were responsible for our emotional and spiritual bankruptcy in later years. If, for example, we had been harshly criticized as children and failed to deal with that reality as adults, we tended to be defensive and insecure. Many of us became walking land mines; the slightest tremor of disapproval could set off an explosion of past pain.

Until we came to terms with the past, it remained a turbid wellspring of anguish, guilt, and shame. Moreover, because the past evoked such negative emotions, we tended to deal with it in negative ways. We either dwelled morbidly in our yesterdays, or we slammed the door and refused to look back.

Eventually, we learned that by shifting perspective, we could transform the past from a severe liability into a valuable asset. Today we use the past to increase our self-awareness—to make new and useful connections between previous occurrences and present problems.

We also use the past as a sort of benchmark. By looking back at what it used to be like, we can easily see how much better it is now, and how far we've come.

THOUGHT FOR TODAY: I choose to use my past as a resource for progress rather than a reservoir for pain.

Coming to Terms with the Past   226

A friend of mine used to relish the fact that we had similar family backgrounds. Whenever we'd meet, he invariably would recount a familiar litany of wrongs committed against him.

When we ran into each other after I hadn't seen him for almost a year, I fully expected more of the same. But to my surprise, he began talking about "what it was like" in an entirely different manner.

"I used to think my past set me apart in some sort of special way," he confided at one point. "I'm sure you remember how I whined about it. Well, around six months ago I started getting out of myself a little bit—I started listening to other people's experiences for a change. And I began to realize that nobody is delivered full-blown into adulthood without some scars, some bad memories, or some residual pain. We've all had crosses to bear.

"I also realized that what did or didn't happen to me is now history," my friend continued, "and I'm learning to deal with it. What really matters is how I live my life today. That's where I still have a choice."

THOUGHT FOR TODAY: Am I ready to leave the past behind and get on with my life?

Coming to Terms with the Past

July 18

For a long time, I carried a lot of guilt for the wrongs I had committed. That painful burden weighed heavily on me, until I became willing to take decisive actions to clear away the wreckage of my past. The most effective of those actions, I found, was making direct amends to the people I had harmed.

Before you make your amends, I was told, be sure you know *why* you're making them—not to punish yourself, but to become free of the past and to further your spiritual growth.

While searching my memory and drawing up an amends list, I tried to focus only on *my* wrongs, rather than on how others had wronged me. In order to learn more about myself, I also tried to pinpoint the character flaws which could have caused my harmful actions.

Perhaps the biggest challenge in the process was overcoming my unwillingness to make certain amends. In several cases I was afraid of the reception I might get; in other instances I rationalized that the amends wasn't really necessary, because I was as much a victim as the person on my list. Thankfully, however, I was able to work through my fear and pride, and was finally able to move forward.

THOUGHT FOR TODAY: Making amends frees me to forgive myself.

Coming to Terms with the Past   228

We're likely to get all sorts of responses when we make direct amends to those we've harmed. Most people will be pleased that we're doing something to turn our lives around, but others, still smarting from our affronts, may respond with sarcasm or even hostility.

Whatever the response, we must not lose sight of the fact that we're making amends to help ourselves. If we have any other motive—trying to get back in someone's good graces, for example, or seeking approval and forgiveness—chances are we'll be disappointed with the results.

How do we benefit when we make amends with the proper motives? It goes without saying that our self-esteem rises when we take actions (especially difficult ones) to improve our lives. In addition, the act of amends often opens the door to self-forgiveness, and can provide the foundation for reconstruction of damaged relationships.

After we make amends to all the people on our list, we experience not only great relief, but also the sense that we are right with ourselves and the world. By coming to terms with the past, we're finally able to live comfortably in the present.

THOUGHT FOR TODAY: I make amends to help myself; the response I receive is of secondary importance.

July 20

The amends process continues in our lives long after we've made face-to-face apologies and restitution. Through our changing attitudes and behavior, one might say that we make "silent amends" each day to our loved ones and others who had been harmed by our past actions.

Where once we were arrogant and contentious, we've become understanding and agreeable. Where once we were selfish and possessive, we now go out of our way to share a newfound happiness. Where once we burdened others with blaming and self-pity, our presence today reflects vitality, emotional wellness, and a determination to live life to its fullest.

Of all our amends, none have been more important than those we've made to ourselves. For years we had created a personal hell; our sense of unworthiness brought about erratic behavior that ultimately harmed us as grievously as it did anyone else.

That is why many of us decided to put our own names at the top of our amends list. Since that time, we've "silently" continued the amends process by giving ourselves the respect, kindness, and love we now feel we deserve.

THOUGHT FOR TODAY: We are making "silent amends" for our past wrongs by the way we live today.

Coming to terms with the past was not something I decided to do one rainy afternoon. The necessity of taking actions along these lines came upon me only gradually, and the actions themselves have continued to this day.

During the first year of recovery, a personal inventory allowed me to see my past as it really was—not as I had always imagined or exaggerated it. Over time much more was revealed: I developed surprising new awarenesses, uncovered a host of unresolved issues, and began to work through character defects I never knew I had. By making amends and taking care of unfinished business, I became free of the guilt and remorse that had haunted me for years.

Along the way I began to understand and apply spiritual principles, which also helped me come to terms with the past. I have learned to forgive others and myself. I have developed faith in God's power to remove the resentments and obsessions that can keep me chained to my previous life. I have built a self-image that is in accord with the realities of today rather than the memories of yesterday.

THOUGHT FOR TODAY: We come to terms with the past not all at once with a single action, but with many actions taken over time.

July 22

Affirmation

The past is now behind me. I have come to terms with yesterday and have no fear of tomorrow. My thoughts and energies are directed to the present—this place, this day, this moment.

Today I neither turn my back on the past nor revisit it morbidly or needlessly. Because I view my previous life from a new vantage point, it no longer has the power to harm or haunt me. On the contrary, my past has become one of my most valued assets.

Certainly it is a storehouse of useful information, which can help me to make new connections and to heighten my self-awareness. If I remember the bitterness and confusion of the past, it is unlikely that I'll ever have to live that way again. Moreover, those memories can aid me in keeping present adversities in perspective; few things these days are as serious as they first might seem.

Because of my past experiences, I have become a more understanding and empathetic person. I can often identify with the pain, life-struggles, and unresolved problems of my fellows, and perhaps be of service.

THOUGHT FOR TODAY: I won't allow myself to forget the past, but neither will I allow its memories to detract from the present.

Coming to Terms with the Past

30

Relationships

By friendship you mean the greatest love, the greatest usefulness, the most open communication, the noblest sufferings, the severest truth, the heartiest counsel, and the greatest union of minds of which brave men and women are capable.

—JEREMY TAYLOR

July 23

Our inner lives have been galvanized by profound and continuing change. Everything is different,
from our motives and reactions to our attitudes, our
values, and especially the way we feel about ourselves.

When we change so dramatically on the inside,
it's bound to affect our interactions with others,
particularly those we've lived with, worked with, or
known for years. If a work association has been built
on false impressions or dishonesty, for example, we
soon find that we have to come clean and rebuild the
relationship—or end it.

If our bond to a brother or sister centers around
mutual roles as victims, we no longer can afford to
participate in the relationship in the same way. The
reason, of course, is that today we're trying to put
aside our "victim" mentality.

Similarly, if our relationship with a parent has
remained at the same level of dependence-
and-control as when we were in grade school, clearly
we need to change our part in it. Here again our goal
is to become responsible, to develop an independent
identity, and to become an individual in our own
right.

THOUGHT FOR TODAY: Relationships must change
in recovery. I pray for the willingness and courage to
bring that about.

I wouldn't admit it to anyone, not even to myself, but I used to desperately envy the closeness and warmth that other people seemed to share with their families and friends.

From time to time I would go out of my way to create those qualities in my own strained relationships. I'd buy presents, arrange special outings, and be on my best behavior. Things would change for a while, or at least I thought they did. However, it was all on the surface; nothing was really different.

I've since learned that the way I relate to others is directly connected to the way I feel about myself. Because I was filled with self-loathing back then, it was all but impossible to have close and loving relationships.

As I became more accepting of myself in recovery, I was able to be more accepting of others. As I became more comfortable in my own skin, I could be more at ease with others. As I began to truly care about myself and act accordingly, I was able to care about others and treat them with kindness, understanding, and love.

THOUGHT FOR TODAY: Before I can improve my relationships with others, I must first improve my relationship with myself.

Relationships

July 25

We couldn't understand why our relationships were so disappointing. Why did people treat us the way they did? Why did they pull back, when we made it clear we needed them? What was the matter with everyone?

We didn't see it then, but we certainly realize now that our extreme self-centeredness was at the root of our difficulties with other people. We almost always thought of ourselves first. We talked about ourselves incessantly. We focused on what others could and should do for us. We insisted on having our own way no matter what the situation or circumstance. Our relationships could withstand only so much of that kind of behavior before they deteriorated and fell apart.

When we broke out of the shell of self-centeredness, our relationships began to improve immeasurably. We learned to listen to others; we considered their feelings and not just our own; we compromised. We became willing to overlook the minor things, and concentrated instead on what was best for the relationship. For the first time in our lives we became sincerely concerned with the wants and needs of others.

THOUGHT FOR TODAY: When I become less self-centered, that's when my relationships will improve.

In recovery, we emerged from the make-believe world of denial and came face to face with our twisted and destructive family relationships. The challenge of rebuilding them—of getting along better with our mothers, fathers, brothers, and sisters—seemed overwhelming.

How could we avoid participating, as we always had, in the power struggles, game-playing, and button-pushing? What could we do when the tension mounted and the sparks flew? Would anything ever change?

When we expressed our discouragement to other recovering people, they urged us not to give up hope. They had faced similar situations and had felt just as frustrated. It had taken a long time, they said, but now their family ties were closer than ever.

Here are some of the suggestions we received.

Put aside all expectations. Don't expect your family to understand your new beliefs, for example, or to change their ways just because you've changed yours.

You may not like what they do and say, but for now try to accept family members as they are. Concentrate less on their actions and more on your own reactions. Above all, be patient—not just with them, but with yourself as well.

THOUGHT FOR TODAY: Let's forget about *their* behavior. What can *I* do, right now, to improve the family relationship?

Relationships

July 27

I reached out for help on a Sunday afternoon. By that evening I had met with more than a dozen recovering people who made it clear that they were willing to do anything in their power to be of service.

For the next week or so, I stayed in close contact and allowed them to care for me. But as soon as I gained a sense of stability, all I wanted to do was break away. "I appreciate what you guys have done for me," I thought, "but I don't need your help anymore."

Looking back, I can see where that attitude came from. Because of my low self-worth and stifling fear of people, the last thing I wanted was close personal involvement.

I soon found out, however, that I couldn't make any real progress in recovery on my own. I needed to interact and build relationships with other recovering people—people who understood what I was going through, because they had been there themselves.

Just about everything I've learned in recovery has come from others. Whatever insights I've gained over the years have been passed along to me. Where once I shunned fellowship and interaction, I now am grateful for it.

THOUGHT FOR TODAY: Recovery didn't begin with me, and neither will it end with me.

Of all our relationships, none is more significant than the one we have with God. Along with the fact that faith in Him has added a new dimension to our lives, many of us also believe that continuing recovery is contingent on the maintenance of our spiritual condition.

Certainly our relationship with God is a highly personal matter that differs for each of us. Regardless of our individual conception and form of expression, however, our faith and trust in a Power greater than ourselves has brought about many miracles in our lives.

With God's help, we have been relieved of our addictions, obsessions, and painful ties to the past.

We turn to God for strength and courage. Knowing that He is with us makes it easier to face our fears and work through our character flaws.

We try to accept whatever happens as part of God's perfect plan. We know that He will fulfill our needs and take care of us in the best possible way.

By seeking knowledge of God's will for us, and praying for the power to carry it out, we have found a whole new purpose and direction in life.

THOUGHT FOR TODAY: I am never alone, for God is with me always.

Relationships

Affirmation

Relationships are central to my life today. Because of my close bonds with others, I no longer am drifting aimlessly. Shared thoughts, feelings, and experiences give substance and real meaning to my existence.

My deepening relationship with God, especially, is bringing about a kaleidoscope of extraordinary changes. Where once fear invaded my every thought, I have found a wellspring of serenity in Him. Where in the past I sowed discord and instigated unrest among my fellows, I now do what I can to foster harmony and stability.

It is my firm belief that God works through people. Through my relationships with others, I continue to gain invaluable knowledge and insights. I have become convinced, because of my own experiences, that we can all be channels for God's grace.

I used to feel that successful relationships were beyond my capability, that harmful ones were my inevitable and immutable lot. To the contrary, I have found that life-enhancing changes within me have revitalized my relationships. It has become possible for me to be a worker among workers, and a friend among friends.

THOUGHT FOR TODAY: Each successful relationship is a reflection of God's grace in my life.

31

Letting Go

Time is like a river of fleeting events, and its current is strong; as soon as something comes into sight, it is swept past us, and something else takes its place, and that too will be swept away.

—MARCUS AURELIUS

July 30

I heard it over and over, dozens and dozens of times, and I just couldn't get it. People in my recovery group would describe bothersome or even critical problems in their lives, then say in all seriousness, "I'm just going to have to let it go."

It sounded so irresponsible, not to mention naive. What did they expect? That if they closed their eyes their problems would disappear? That their troubles would simply evaporate?

It was quite some time before I really *listened* to what they were saying, and began to understand the actual meaning of "letting go and letting God."

As I apply it in my own life today, letting go and letting God is what I do after I've taken all possible steps to resolve a problem on my own. It means accepting my limitations, and in most cases my powerlessness, and then figuratively putting down the burden I've been carrying.

Letting go and letting God also means trying to disentangle myself emotionally, in order to clear the channel to God. It means releasing my problem, with faith and trust that He will provide the solution.

THOUGHT FOR TODAY: Have I done all I can? Is it time to let go and let God?

We can't help being a little embarrassed when we remember how the need for approval controlled our lives. It influenced our thoughts, opinions, and just about everything we did.

The need to be liked, admired, respected, and accepted by everyone was one of the hardest things to let go of in recovery. And for good reason. We had been that way all of our lives. We were fragile, fearful, and insecure. We needed all the strokes we could get; in fact, we depended on them for what little self-esteem we had.

Building self-esteem from within, rather than from the outside—that remains a primary challenge in recovery. We try to do what is right for us, to make choices based on our own personal wants, likes, and needs—from clothing styles to career decisions. We try to know and be ourselves.

To make all of that possible, we've had to really concentrate on letting go of the idea that we're not "okay" unless we have the approval of others. Come to think of it, outside approval never made any *real* difference in our lives—inside approval, on the other hand, has made all the difference.

THOUGHT FOR TODAY: I will release myself from the illusion that I need other people's approval to be happy.

Letting Go

August 1

When we realize it's necessary to let something go, yet are unable to do so, fear is what usually keeps us from loosening our grip. Never was that more apparent than when we were beginning our new life.

It had already become clear that we would be well advised to let go of many of the things that sustained us in our old life: an image bound up with material pursuits and possessions; character defects that were still "working" for us; dependencies on people, things, and substances.

But we couldn't let go completely, because we feared what might happen to us. We were afraid that we would lose our identity, that we'd become boring, that people wouldn't like us. We were afraid of taking risks, meeting new people, trying and perhaps failing. We were afraid of change and the unknown.

Over time—a day at a time—we were able to put fear behind us. What made it possible was the growing realization that we weren't just letting things go and leaving empty spaces. We were replacing self-centered pursuits with spiritual goals, pride with humility, and fear with faith.

THOUGHT FOR TODAY: When I let go of the old, I make room for the new.

Letting Go   244

We've all been there. It's been proved to us beyond any doubt that what we're trying to fix is irreparable, that where we're heading is the wrong direction, that what we're obsessed with is out of our hands. Yet, like a dog shaking a rag doll, we stubbornly hang on and keep doing what we've been doing.

We know what happens to us when we refuse to let go. We develop tunnel vision, becoming so focused on our own limited objectives that we're blind to any other possibilities. We're motivated not by positive traits, but by character defects such as closed-mindedness and willfulness.

By not letting go, we tend to exacerbate whatever is going on, compounding our frustration, anxiety, and pain. Because we can't see or won't heed the caution signs, we end up with something that just isn't right for us.

When we finally do let go, we wonder what took us so long. We wish we could have done it sooner, because the difference in the way we feel is so dramatic. Well, perhaps next time . . .

THOUGHT FOR TODAY: By remaining aware of my limitations as well as my capabilities, I'll know when it's time to let go.

August 3

My relationship with her had been over for months. She was deeply involved with someone else. But the breakup was still tearing me apart; I couldn't get her out of my mind.

I tried—heaven knows I tried—to get over her. I worked hard at stripping away any illusions I might have that we could be back together. I did everything I could to accept things as they were, and to stop wishing or pretending that they were different.

I reminded myself again and again that I was powerless over her, over the way things had turned out, and even over the way I had been feeling since she left. Yet no matter what I did, I still couldn't let go.

In the end, I turned to God. I asked Him in my prayers for the strength to let her go, since that seemed to be His will. I asked Him to ease my heartache. I asked Him to help me become open to another way, a better way, His way.

Days and weeks went by. Gradually, I was able to release her and the relationship. I couldn't do it all at once, but eventually, with God's help, I was finally able to let go.

THOUGHT FOR TODAY: Letting go is an affirmative act of faith.

August 4

When other people from dysfunctional families opened up to us, it became relatively easy to let go of the idea that we were different. They talked about themselves and it was as if they were telling our story.

Once we gave up the idea that we were unique, we could accept help and devote our attention to freeing ourselves of other destructive illusions.

We were able to let go

. . . of the illusion that our parents' perception of us was accurate. ("You're worthless, just like your father . . . .")

. . . of the belief that we came into recovery with a realistic self-image. ("I'm sick, suffering, and second-rate . . . .")

. . . of survival roles from the past. ("If I don't look out for myself, who will?")

. . . of misconceptions and false values we grew up with. ("It's okay as long as you don't get caught . . . .")

. . . of the need to punish and blame our parents. ("I'll show them. Someday they'll get theirs . . . .")

. . . of the conviction that we had no choices. ("I can't help it, I'll always be this way . . . .")

THOUGHT FOR TODAY: Am I still hanging on to destructive illusions?

Letting Go

August 5

I choose not to squander my time and energy on things I cannot change. My serenity is too dear to sacrifice on circumstances beyond my control.

When I have done all I can, I will let go and let God. I will accept my limitations and my powerlessness. I will try to disentangle myself emotionally in order to clear the channel to my Higher Power.

If I am still having difficulty letting go, I will ask God to give me the courage and strength I need. I will ask Him to show me what He would have me be and do.

When I am ready to release illusions, dependencies, or character defects, I will try to put aside any lingering misgivings I may have. Faith—the faith that already has replaced many of my fears—tells me that the "empty spaces" within will be filled. Their new contents will be in accord with God's plan for good in my life.

It is deeply comforting to know that I need only do my part, taking the responsibility that is mine. I can then leave the rest in the best hands possible—God's hands.

THOUGHT FOR TODAY: When I let go, the struggle ends.

32

Maturity

Everybody wants to be somebody; nobody wants to grow.

—GOETHE

August 6

There once was a computer programmer who had extraordinary skills. He had always been able to get top jobs, but had never been able to keep them. The problem was his immature behavior.

When anyone criticized him or even questioned his methods, he would become extremely upset and defensive. If he didn't get his way, he would fly into a tantrum. He often refused to do things he felt were beneath him.

"I was impossible to work with," he says. "I would get so intolerant that I'd sometimes become abusive. It's no wonder I kept getting fired."

At one point his supervisor gave him an ultimatum: Either go to the company's employee assistance counselor for help, or be terminated. He chose to go into counseling. After a few sessions, the counselor suggested that his inability to get along with others was a reflection of his emotional immaturity.

"That was a hard truth to swallow," he says. "As usual I reacted defensively. Eventually, though, I admitted that the problem wasn't with 'them,' but with me. I was able to see that my immaturity was interfering not only with my ability to get along with others and keep a job, but with the way I fitted into the world."

THOUGHT FOR TODAY: Are the problems I'm having due to immature behavior on my part?

We began our new lives when we were eighteen years old—or twenty-seven, or forty-two, or sixty-five. Most of us "looked" our age and, accordingly, people expected us to "act" our age. But there was a catch: Although we had matured physically and intellectually, many of us had not kept pace emotionally.

We had the physical development of adults, with the underdeveloped emotions of teenagers. We were self-conscious and fearful around other people, and it was difficult for us to build and maintain relationships. It took very little to hurt our feelings, and we frequently exaggerated or lied to make ourselves look good. Our volatility and inappropriate behavior often surprised those around us.

At first we were ashamed that we had "failed" to mature emotionally. But we soon understood that we were immature for good reason. Our emotional growth had been stunted by our addictions, by our overdependence on others, and by our dysfunctional family situations.

We never really had a chance to grow up—to learn how to interact with others and make our way smoothly through the world. When it was suggested in early recovery that our lives were unmanageable, we could hardly disagree.

THOUGHT FOR TODAY: There is no reason to feel "less than" just because I temporarily lack certain social skills.

August 8

When we realized just how immature we were, many of us felt overwhelmed. It seemed unlikely that we would ever catch up. As with so many other fundamental changes, however, maturity came to us a day at a time, and as the result of many actions and experiences.

We began to grow by doing what was in front of us, without running away. Instead of immediately quitting a job that became difficult, for example, we learned to walk through the fear and discomfort—and matured by doing so. Instead of breaking up a relationship that felt "too close," we tried to become more open and vulnerable—and matured in the process.

We also gained maturity by taking responsibility for our actions on a daily basis; by acknowledging mistakes and shortcomings; and by making amends. In addition, and perhaps most important, we worked hard at becoming rigorously self-honest at all times and in all situations.

When we wondered aloud after several months if we were ever going to make real progress in becoming more mature, our friends assured us, with unmistakable sincerity, that we already had.

THOUGHT FOR TODAY: I will do what is in front of me. I won't sidestep or run away.

Looking back, it seems amazing that I didn't see my erratic and childish behavior for what it was. It certainly must have been obvious to everyone else.

My usual *modus operandi* was immediate gratification. No matter what I had, it was never enough; I always craved more. More alcohol, more money, more security, more approval.

As further evidence of my immaturity, I reacted with outrage to even imagined affronts; carried resentments until they grew white-hot within me; and refused to ever forgive anyone. All of those traits, of course, contributed greatly to my inability to cope with life on life's terms.

The primary manifestation of my immaturity, however, was my lack of humility and preoccupation with self. Just about everything I did was designed for my personal satisfaction. My relationships and interactions—even with my own family members— were often structured around my need to look good, or other benefits I might receive.

In those days, ironically, I thought of myself as highly mature, not to mention sophisticated and erudite. I had no idea, when I began my recovery, that immaturity was one of my biggest problems.

THOUGHT FOR TODAY: As I become less self-centered, I become more mature.

August 10

The spiritual way of life has made it possible for us to become mature in ways we could not have imagined. Most of the time, our behavior and reactions reflect the inner peace and security we have gained. We can face and deal with life's changes and challenges. We are stable and sure of ourselves.

How did this come about? What's the connection between spirituality and maturity?

When we first learn about spiritual principles, we see that they offer solutions to our living problems. We soon begin to apply these principles day by day, with good results.

In a typical scenario, our initial impulse when affronted may be to strike back, to get even, to become resentful. Instead, we stop ourselves and try to respond maturely—with understanding, patience, and self-restraint—to whatever has provoked us.

Over time, the connection that we may not have seen earlier becomes quite clear. By practicing spiritual principles in our responses and our actions—by shifting focus from ourselves to others and God—we are able to move steadily from immaturity to maturity.

THOUGHT FOR TODAY: The spiritual path leads to greater maturity.

The hallmarks of my life today include a growing acceptance of myself as I am, plus a true sense of equality with my brothers and sisters. These new realities provide tangible evidence that I have become more mature.

In the past, my immaturity compelled me to constantly compare myself to others. I saw life as a ladder on which I invariably stood a rung above or a rung below my fellows. I felt "better than" or "less than," but never "equal to."

Those endless comparisons led me into intense competitiveness. If I felt that someone was more capable than I (on a higher rung), I would do my best to reverse our positions, or knock them off the ladder. I would also compete with someone I felt was less capable (on a lower rung), in order to strengthen my own position.

Life was an ongoing battle in which I was always a loser, no matter how well or poorly I competed.

Because of my increasing self-acceptance, I now rarely feel the need to compare or compete. I gratefully acknowledge my God-given capabilities, and most of the time strive only for further personal and spiritual growth.

THOUGHT FOR TODAY: The level of my self-acceptance is a good gauge of my maturity.

August 12

Affirmation

My goal is to become a more mature person, not only in the ways I interact with others, but also as I relate to myself.

Above all else, the practice of spiritual principles will bring me closer to this goal. Each time I respond with patience rather than impatience, with understanding rather than judgment, and with forgiveness rather than resentment, I will gain maturity.

I affirm that I am neither greater than nor less than my fellows, but equal to them. To strengthen this belief, I will strive to truly accept myself as I am. The more self-acceptance I achieve, the less tempted I will be to immaturely compare myself to others.

Today I will help myself grow by faithfully doing what is in front of me, even if that means walking through fear or pain. I will take full responsibility for my actions, admitting mistakes and acknowledging shortcomings, while also graciously accepting praise.

I am grateful that my increasing maturity is helping me to shift focus from myself to God's larger world, and to accept life on life's terms.

THOUGHT FOR TODAY: Maturity won't develop by force of will, but as the result of choices I make and actions I take.

33

Self-will

*Self-will is so ardent and active, that it will break a
world to pieces, to make a stool to sit on.*

—RICHARD CECIL

August 13

It's doubtful that the phrase "self-will" ever crossed my mind, let alone my lips, during my old life. In a way this is surprising, considering that self-will was such a destructive force in virtually everything I did.

The way I saw it, my combined resources of intellect, talent, and willpower were all I needed to run my life successfully—to achieve everything I believed I was meant to achieve in the grand scheme of things. Self-sufficiency would be my golden passport to a very special destiny.

Needless to say, few things worked out in accordance with my willful plans and designs. My misguided philosophy caused me to live in a state of frustration, disappointment, and anger. At the end, I was a broken man, filled with self-doubt yet still wondering where I'd gone wrong. I was convinced, bone-deep, that since I was responsible for my destiny, I had failed.

If there was any failure, it was in my inability to see that the quality I valued and relied on the most was the one that served me least. Self-will was not the solution to my problems, but their cause.

THOUGHT FOR TODAY: Isn't the responsibility of playing God somewhat beyond my capability?

Self-will 258

There came a time, a very special time, when we made a decision to turn our will and our life over to the care of God. For some of us, the decision was spurred by a sharp awareness that our lives lacked direction, that we were purposeless and unhappy. Others among us made the decision because of addictive despair, because of a spiritual awakening, or by virtue of finally wanting something better.

Regardless of how we arrived at the decision to seek and do God's will, most of us were somewhat confused and even apprehensive about how best to put our resolve into action. It was all so new and mysterious, so contrary to the way we had lived in the past.

But we soon found that all we needed to open the door was the key of willingness. We prayed and we meditated, and in small ways at first we began to trust our growing intuition. When we reached a crossroad or faced a dilemma, it became increasingly easy to rely on God's guidance. As time went on, we found ways to strengthen our bond with God, and to develop a clearer sense of His will for us.

THOUGHT FOR TODAY: Each day I will renew my decision to try to align my will with God's will.

Self-will

August 15

"It's almost as if I'm starting all over again with God," a woman I know was telling me. "On one level it seems strange, because He's been part of my world as far back as I can remember. But on another level, my new relationship with Him will probably turn out to be what I can best describe as a reawakening."

She went on to remind me of her religious upbringing and strong commitment to her church. "But even with all that involvement, I felt anxious and demoralized a lot of the time. I was unfulfilled and empty inside. Most of all, I felt lost.

"It went on like that for some time," she continued. "Then, one morning I had a profound realization. It became clear to me that despite all my knowledge, and despite all my religious activities, I had always kept God on the fringes. What really propelled me through life was my own self-will.

"That was my awakening," my friend said. "I had never really included God in my life in a personal way. I had never allowed myself to be loved and guided by Him. That's what I mean when I say I'm starting again with God."

THOUGHT FOR TODAY· Thy will, not mine, be done.

Self-will run riot—that's how we behaved for a long time. Some of us were like raging bulls. We lowered our heads and literally butted our way through life, single-mindedly focused on what we needed, what we wanted, what we coveted.

Others among us, although no less willful, were sometimes able to mask our self-seeking motives. We manipulatively convinced others and even ourselves that our actions were right, necessary, and best for all concerned.

In either case, our tremendous need to control and prevail blinded us to what was truly beneficial. We ended up hurting many people emotionally and spiritually. And we injured ourselves, because our unyielding self-will shut us off from the loving kindness of God's will. If we thought of Him at all, it was during times of utter desperation.

Providentially, all of that has changed. Our self-will has diminished, and our focus has widened. Today we see that God's will involves far more than seeking and receiving His guidance during times of crisis. We believe there are opportunities to joyfully do His will each day—by being kind, by being loving, by being giving, by being forgiving.

THOUGHT FOR TODAY: I will hold fast to the reality that God's will for me is happiness, joy, and freedom.

Self-will

August 17

There are times, usually when things are going along on an even keel, when I temporarily forget that God is responsible for all the goodness in my life. Self-will then begins to take root. If I don't stop in time, I push Him out of my mind entirely and start trying to run the show myself.

Sometimes I lapse into self-will in another way. I usually don't hesitate to seek God's wisdom and strength concerning serious matters such as personal illness, a strained relationship with a loved one, or a pivotal career decision. But on a day-to-day basis, when facing routine activities and interactions, I have a tendency to willfully take charge without even considering what God would have me do.

I certainly don't expect myself to turn my will and life over to God's care in all situations and at all times; my goal is spiritual progress, not spiritual perfection. It is important, however, that I have a sincere willingness to do so for the most part. There's simply no question about it: My days are far more successful and serene when I try to seek and do God's will, than when I follow the dictates of my own.

THOUGHT FOR TODAY: I may not always be successful, but my continuing goal is to seek and do God's will.

There is hardly a greater challenge for any of us than to have healthy, happy, and productive relationships. We know from experience that few things are more satisfying than to have harmonious bonds with loved ones, as well as those with whom we interact on a daily basis.

As we all know, it's far easier to get along when we're kind and courteous than when we're thoughtless and disrespectful. Less obvious, however, is the harmony that can be achieved in relationships when we try to keep our willfulness in check.

If we stop and think about it, most friction in relationships occurs when we insist on getting our way—when we try to manage and control everything from routine conversations to major decisions.

But of course, people have their own ideas, and naturally we don't always get our way. So we become disappointed and angry; invariably, the relationship is harmed.

The way to avoid such problems, we've found, is to try to keep our will in perspective and balance. We can best do this by staying sensitive to the needs, wants, and ideas of others; by seeking compromises that are mutually beneficial; and by working for a loving give-and-take.

THOUGHT FOR TODAY: Whenever I try to exert my will over someone else, the relationship is bound to suffer.

Self-will

August 19

Affirmation

I affirm my decision once again to turn my will and life over to the care of God. As time goes on, it becomes easier to know and trust what He would have me do, and to move into action accordingly.

My intellect, talent, and willpower, for example, are gifts with great positive potential. I have learned from experience that they can be used most productively when they are applied along the lines of God's will rather than my own. I affirm in my mind and heart that God has the wisdom, vision, and design for the greatest good.

In the same way, my relationships are bound to be healthier and more harmonious when I remember that it is God's will for me to be kind, understanding, compassionate, and giving with others.

I affirm that God's love is available to me at all times and in all places, throughout this and every day of my life. I need not wait for a time of desperation— nor for a situation I cannot handle on my own—before I turn to Him for wisdom, guidance, and strength.

THOUGHT FOR TODAY: I will set aside my will in favor of God's will. I will be a conduit for His good.

34

Honesty

Without seeking, truth cannot be known at all. It can neither be declared from pulpits, nor set down in articles, nor in any wise prepared and sold in packages ready for use. Truth must be ground for every man by himself out of its husk, with such help as he can get, indeed, but not without stern labor of his own.

—JOHN RUSKIN

August 20

When I was out there in that world of addiction and terror, dishonesty was second nature to me—it was as automatic as breathing in and out. Not only had I developed deeply grooved habits of lying while growing up in a dysfunctional family, but my subsequent alcoholism necessitated even more intricate webs of deceit.

There were the ego-generated lies, designed to win favor while camouflaging the real me. There were the everyday lies used to cover up, alibi, or deny my irresponsible behavior. And there were the lies which spewed forth reflexively when it would have been just as easy to tell the truth.

Honesty in all its dimensions—that's what has become second nature in my life today. One reason is that my relationships and actions are such that there's no need for dishonesty. More importantly, when I'm less than honest I quickly become extremely uncomfortable—and I can no longer abide that feeling. It comes down to the fact that when I'm honest I feel good about myself, and when I'm dishonest the opposite is true.

THOUGHT FOR TODAY: Honesty will become the underlying structure of my life today.

As we work to build self-esteem, it quickly becomes clear that self-honesty is an invaluable tool for progress. In fact, it's the one tool we cannot do without. When we finally became willing to look at our true feelings and the shredded fabric of our lives, it was self-honesty that brought us into recovery.

The people we met didn't remain strangers for long. They shared honestly and openly about themselves, and we were soon encouraged to do the same. When we began to talk about the personal insights we were gaining through self-honesty, the results were phenomenal.

As if by magic, our feelings, fears, and conflicts lost their power to cause us pain. At the same time, the honesty and responsibility involved in revealing our hidden selves went a long way toward restoring our self-esteem.

Because of self-honesty and openness, we're free to be ourselves today. The energy we once devoted to secretiveness and denial can now be used to further the process of self-discovery, to improve our relationships with others, and to grow spiritually.

THOUGHT FOR TODAY: I will share my secrets and drain them of their power.

Broken promises, denial, excuses, exaggerations—lies upon lies upon lies. That's how many of us grew up. In our households, fiction rather than fact was the norm. We wouldn't have recognized truth if it stared us in the eye.

Our parents lied to each other and for each other. It seemed that they preferred lies to truths, and we followed right along. The whole family lied to hide or sidestep drunkenness, violence, irresponsibility, or other unpleasant realities. We as youngsters lied to get attention, to avoid punishment, to survive.

If we didn't grow out of these ingrained habit patterns, we paid a heavy price as adults. Because our lies became even more widespread, it was impossible to keep track of them. We feared getting caught, and often it was unavoidable. People stopped trusting and respecting us; worse, we no longer trusted or respected ourselves.

Needless to say, it's exceedingly difficult to break these lifelong habits; we feel naked and vulnerable without our armor of deceit. Yet we want to move forward, and we know that our ability to function in the world will be severely limited if we don't take actions to become honest and aboveboard in all our affairs.

THOUGHT FOR TODAY: There were times when it seemed that dishonesty made life simpler. I've since learned that nothing is more simple than the truth.

When we were dishonest in the past, we rarely gave it a second thought. But when we lie or even stretch the truth these days, it's a far different story. We feel guilty and embarrassed, certainly, but more than anything we're disappointed with ourselves.

If dishonesty continues to be a problem, what actions can you take to help yourself? First, the decision to stop lying ought to be given the priority it deserves. One of the best ways to do this is to discuss the matter openly, keeping a trusted friend apprised of your ongoing progress or the lack of it.

Approach the problem only a day at a time. That way, you need not burden yourself with the unrealistic goal of becoming and remaining totally honest "forever."

It can be extremely useful, at the end of each day, to log any incidents of dishonesty. By spelling out the circumstances, your feelings at the time, your reasons, and so on, you can gain further awareness of the whys and wherefores of your problem. And when you've had a "successful" day, don't forget to make note of that also, paying special attention to how good it felt to be honest.

THOUGHT FOR TODAY: Just for today, I will strive to be completely honest.

August 24

From childhood into adulthood, from sickness into health, my mind has never completely stopped lying to me about myself. Even after I had traveled far toward emotional and spiritual wellness, a self-deprecating voice continued to pursue me relentlessly.

When I puzzled over the causes of my parents' hostile treatment of me, for example, my mind would do its best to evoke feelings of guilt: "If you had been a better son . . ." No matter what I accomplished, my mind would hatch a falsehood to tear me down.

To this day, I must be on guard against those cunningly diabolical lies that can hurt me the most: "A drink would fix it . . . ." "What's all this God stuff? He doesn't even know you're alive . . . ."

Over the years I have learned that I must deal with these attacks promptly, before they can cause serious harm. It's important at certain times to override my mind, so to speak, in order to separate truth from lie and reality from unreality. It's necessary then to consciously and assertively replace the false messages with accurate and self-affirming ones.

THOUGHT FOR TODAY: I will take a stand against dishonesty, especially from myself about myself.

One of the greatest challenges in our new life is to remain rigorously self-honest. But as we all know, it's far more difficult to avoid dishonesty with ourselves than it is with others. That's why ongoing self-appraisal is so important; the more layers we peel away, the more unconscious self-deception we're likely to uncover.

When we discover startling new truths about ourselves and our backgrounds, we may sometimes be tempted to "let sleeping dogs lie." Or we may chastise ourselves for not making the discoveries sooner. But those feelings do pass, for we know that ever-deeper levels of self-honesty are essential if we are to continue growing emotionally and spiritually.

In practical terms, self-honesty leads to heightened awareness and, in turn, to the possibility of positive changes in our attitudes and actions. If on the other hand we continue to deceive ourselves, we will never change.

It is axiomatic that truth is reality. The more we strive to think, feel, and act truthfully, the better able we are to think, feel, and act realistically. By remaining dedicated to the truth in this manner, we're better equipped to choose the right paths and make the right decisions.

THOUGHT FOR TODAY: The rewards of self-honesty are well worth working for.

August 26

Affirmation

I affirm the inestimable value of honesty in my life today. When I am temporarily blown off course by unexpected events or seeming adversity, an honest appraisal of the situation can keep me anchored in reality. So long as I am honest with myself, with others, and with God, I can weather any storm.

Through honest self-evaluation, I am learning a great deal about myself. The deeper I dig and the more truths I unearth, the better equipped I am to accept and initiate change.

My dedication to truth enhances my self-esteem. What a relief it is to put aside the masks and camouflage of yesterday and be the real me. How good it makes me feel when I am able to talk openly and honestly about my fears and foibles, when I can share a secret or admit a mistake.

Honesty in its various dimensions has done much to improve my relationships with family, friends, and coworkers. I once felt it was too complicated to tell the truth, and of course the exact opposite is the case. Life is so much simpler now that everyone knows where I stand and what I'm about.

THOUGHT FOR TODAY: If at times it seems difficult to know God's will, I can be certain that complete honesty is a step in the right direction.

35

Self-pity

Discontent is like ink poured into water, which fills the whole fountain full of blackness. It casts a cloud over the mind, and renders it more occupied about the evil which disquiets than about the means of removing it.

—OWEN FELLTHAM

August 27

We wore our self-pity like medals—Purple Hearts for emotional wounds received. We had grown accustomed to feeling misunderstood and unloved. We felt we were entitled to self-pity; we had a right to feel sorry for ourselves, considering what we had been through.

Even when we began to take responsibility for our lives in recovery, we continued to feel singled out and on the receiving end of an inordinate share of pain and problems. That's how oppressed we were by our prison of self-pity.

It's taken a long time to develop the self-honesty and willingness required to break free of those attitudinal bonds. But we've been able to do so a day at a time, and it's been worth the wait and effort.

Today when we face challenges or adversities, we're able to take them on or walk through them. We seek solutions to our problems and do what is necessary to move forward and get on with the business of living. When we temporarily slip back into self-pity, we quickly take action to extricate ourselves.

Above all, we have strong and abiding faith that God is always with us, providing limitless care and protection no matter how difficult our circumstances.

THOUGHT FOR TODAY: Do I have the self-honesty and willingness to release myself from the prison of self-pity?

It's impossible to remember the names of all the doctors I visited, or the countless medications I tried, to get rid of the depressions that plagued me for years. No matter who I saw or what I took, they came back again and again.

When I once read that Winston Churchill referred to his incapacitating depressions as "the black dog," I knew exactly what he meant. My depressions seemed to come out of nowhere and followed me everywhere.

A year or so into recovery, I became aware for the first time that my depressions were not quite as mysterious as I had believed. I realized that, to a large extent, they were born out of self-pity. As soon as I accepted that fact, my depressions lessened both in frequency and intensity.

Gradually I was able to piece together the typical sequence of events. The starting point was self-pity. "Poor me" would soon lead to "Why me?"—and then to "What's the use?" From there it was only a short haul into full-scale depression.

I hardly ever get depressed anymore. That seems miraculous, but it's probably because I'm able to put a lid on my self-pity before it gets out of hand.

THOUGHT FOR TODAY: "Poor me" is often a starting point for depression.

August 29

We're not particularly proud of the self-pity we feel from time to time. That's why we're less candid about it than we are about most other emotions. We even tend to embellish reality to "justify" feeling sorry for ourselves. If, for example, we are filled with self-pity because our partner has been out of sorts, we're likely to characterize him or her as an unmitigated ogre.

In any case, retreating into self-pity is a choice we do sometimes make when it suits our purposes. We may choose self-pity so as not to confront or deal with our true feelings—our anger, fear, or envy. Similarly, we may opt for self-pity when we're unwilling to accept our powerlessness over a person or situation.

When we choose self-pity, we can avoid taking responsibility. We don't have to look at ourselves honestly, admit our character defects, place our faith and trust in God, or seek solutions.

When we choose self-pity, we often get sympathy from others. Nothing is expected or required from us. We don't have to do anything but wallow in our own misery.

THOUGHT FOR TODAY: Self-pity is not an escape from problems. It *is* a problem.

Some years ago I was unhappy with the results of a legal dispute in which I had been involved. I felt extremely sorry for myself and for weeks made my woes known to anyone who would listen.

Most of my friends were sympathetic. After a while, however, one of them told me it was time to end the "pity-party" and start getting my life back in order. He strongly suggested that I write an inventory on self-pity.

I agreed to do so, partly because I believed any admissions would be tempered by the "special conditions" of my life. Needless to say, I discovered that one's background and circumstances have little to do with the degree of harm invariably caused by this pernicious character defect.

These are some of the things I learned from my inventory.

Self-pity ran through my life's experiences like a corrosive thread.

The more I indulged in self-pity, the more self-obsessed I became.

Self-pity inevitably brought me unhappiness and alienation from those who cared about me.

As long as I felt sorry for myself, nothing changed for the better.

THOUGHT FOR TODAY: Self-pity magnifies the problem while obscuring the solution.

August 31

Like everybody else, I sometimes indulge in self-pity. It doesn't have to be about anything major; most often, in fact, it's the result of something relatively inconsequential such as car trouble, a delayed airline flight, or perhaps even a sore throat.

I tend to forget that I can feel just as sorry for myself over a minor inconvenience as a major problem. That's the thing about self-pity—it has more to do with the intensity of my reaction to an event than the magnitude of the event itself.

These days I no longer consider self-pity a safe harbor; it provides neither refuge nor solace. Indeed, just the opposite is true. When I feel sorry for myself for any length of time, I become extremely uncomfortable. That's why I try to get out of the grip of self-pity as quickly as possible.

The most effective way, I find, is to give thought to those things in my life for which I'm grateful. I think about the blessings of physical and emotional well-being, of days filled with freedom and opportunity, of how fortunate I am to have a loving God in my life.

THOUGHT FOR TODAY: Gratitude for God's blessings is an effective antidote for self-pity.

We've come to realize that all character defects, to one degree or another, mirror self-centeredness. Self-pity, in particular, reflects such a glaring preoccupation with self that it all but blinds us to the larger world.

In the past when we were full of self-pity, we were so involved with our own suffering that we weren't aware of much else. It was difficult for us to show interest in other people—to be genuinely concerned about them and the events in their lives. Because of our limited perspective, we didn't have the opportunity to learn about and practice spiritual principles—to be kind, patient, thoughtful, compassionate, and giving.

By focusing single-mindedly on our personal trials and tribulations, we lost sight of the broad horizons and changing vistas of God's world. For years we missed the majesty of His works. We may have seen but never truly appreciated the colors and harmonies of nature, the cycles and seasons of life, the miracles of faith.

Now that we are trying to replace self-pity with gratitude, and self-centeredness with service to others, we have the chance to live an expansive and very special life—a spiritual life.

THOUGHT FOR TODAY: Am I as concerned about others as I am about myself?

September 2

Affirmation

Now that I have learned about the destructive effects of self-pity, I can no longer justify feeling sorry for myself. Self-pity will only make life's challenges more difficult. It is emotional quicksand and hardly a place to which I can safely retreat.

When I face seeming adversity, I will not slip into self-pity. I will instead affirm my faith and trust in God, reminding myself that He is an ever-present force for good in my life. God has a perfect design for my destiny and He will take care of me, no matter what. I need only be willing to avail myself of His wisdom and strength.

Today I choose constructive ways. I confront and deal with my true feelings. I walk through my pain, seeking solutions and taking actions when called for. I acknowledge my powerlessness and try to accept those things I cannot change.

I will avoid the seductive trap of self-pity by remaining grateful for God's many blessings in my life. He always has and always will meet my every need.

THOUGHT FOR TODAY: If I truly believe in God's plan for my good, how can I harbor feelings of self-pity?

36

Communication

Words are both better and worse than thoughts; they express them, and add to them; they give them power for good and evil; they start them on an endless flight, for instruction and comfort and blessing, or for injury and sorrow and ruin.

—TRYON EDWARDS

September 3

It's been a while, but the images are still etched sharply in our minds. Dad passes out after being in a drunken rage, and not a word is said about his behavior. We come home from school bursting with pride, and as usual no one wants to hear about it. We have a serious problem, and instead of guidance we get the same old guilt-provoking, salt-in-the-wound message: "I blame myself for the way you turned out."

If there was a common denominator in our dysfunctional families, clearly it was the lack of honest and open communication. What exchanges there were tended to be manipulative, confusing, and hostile.

Those were the influences that shaped our ability to communicate. No wonder there was such disharmony and tension in so many of our relationships.

Learning to be better communicators is a continuing challenge, but we're making progress. We're putting aside the negative influences of the past and learning from scratch. We're communicating in ways that clear the air instead of causing pain. We're being as honest and straightforward as we can. We're trying to bring the spirit of love and caring into what we say and how we say it.

THOUGHT FOR TODAY: Do I say what I mean, and mean what I say?

There's been an enormous improvement in all of our relationships now that we're communicating our thoughts, feelings, and opinions in healthy and constructive ways.

Where once we retreated and sulked following an argument, we're now more willing to put our pride behind us and make the first move toward reconciliation.

We often avoided friends if a tragedy had occurred in their lives, because we felt uncomfortable and didn't know what to say. Today we realize the importance of reaching out to those in pain with kindness, caring, and love.

We used to let things go unsaid and allow them to fester within us. Today we recognize that others cannot read our minds; they can only know what we've told them. When there's conflict in our relationships these days, we take steps right away to deal with it.

When parents pushed our buttons in the past, we got angry and fought back. Now we try to exercise self-restraint by calmly letting them know how we feel, and then going on to something else.

Our language skills always seemed inadequate to express what we felt. We've come to see that while words are important, so too are facial expressions, gestures, and even silence. A smile or gentle touch can be as articulate and reassuring as anything we say.

THOUGHT FOR TODAY: I have choices in the way I communicate my thoughts and feelings.

September 5

At certain times during the lunar cycle, extremely low tides uncover a reef that is usually submerged along the coastline near my home. I can walk out and look into tide pools filled with marine organisms of all kinds. Especially fascinating are the sea anemones, flowerlike creatures that close up when they are touched or sense they are about to be touched.

That's the way many of us used to be—we withdrew into ourselves when we felt someone was getting too close. The connection was clear: People caused pain.

Thankfully, today we're no longer afraid to stay open to others. Because we have greater self-worth and are more sure of ourselves, we don't cringe reflexively when somebody says the "wrong thing." We've learned to see thoughtless remarks or insinuations for what they are; we consider the source, and rarely take such things personally anymore.

Besides that, when we allow ourselves to be open and vulnerable, we enjoy the warmth and security of close relationships, as well as the intimacy of shared experiences. We have a true sense of belonging and are becoming increasingly convinced that God does indeed work through people.

THOUGHT FOR TODAY: I will try to open up just a little bit more today.

We all know what it's like to be talking with someone and suddenly become aware that they are not listening. The look on their face tells us that their mind is elsewhere, or that they're formulating what they are going to say just as soon as we pause for breath.

Naturally, we feel bad when this happens. We know from personal experience that few things threaten our self-esteem more than indifference. On the other hand, when someone listens to us attentively, we know that they care, and we tend to feel good about ourselves.

Indeed, the friends we value most are the ones who really listen to us; we're drawn to people who are interested in hearing what we have to say. Similarly, those drawn to us are influenced by the sense that we're interested in their lives.

In the past, if we listened at all it was only to those people "worth listening to." We've since become less self-centered and more sensitive to the feelings of others. We try to listen to everyone with whom we come in contact, and we believe that every person is important.

THOUGHT FOR TODAY: For open, honest, and caring communication, listening is perhaps more important than talking.

Communication

September 7

We spent a good part of our lives preoccupied with self. Hardly an hour passed when we weren't thinking primarily of ourselves, and how the actions or inactions of others might affect our lives. Our thoughts revolved almost exclusively around *our* plans, *our* problems, *our* wants, *our* needs.

As we've matured and begun to live a spiritual life, we've found that the hours we pass in this way are uncomfortable, unproductive, and exhausting. We've also found that real happiness and personal fulfillment comes from being of service to others.

One of the best ways to serve another person, and at the same time reduce our self-involvement, is to become a good listener. We listen best, we find, when we try to hear the feelings behind the words— when we go beyond simple attentiveness and listen understandingly, empathetically, and nonjudgmentally.

Even when we are unable to come up with specific advice or helpful answers, a caring nod of the head or "I know" can make a difference. Listening is a gift of kindness we can always offer to another person.

THOUGHT FOR TODAY: Listening attentively to others is a sure way out of self-involvement.

I was one of those people who found it painfully difficult to talk to others. I was fearful and insecure, and I had a desperate need to look good. Those feelings, combined with a lack of communication skills, made conversation a highly stressful undertaking. I avoided it whenever possible.

Considering how much I suffered because of my inability to communicate, I'm most grateful that those days are behind me. Today it's easy—almost natural—for me to talk openly and honestly about myself, and to listen receptively when others do the same.

This change took place over a period of years. It involved more than overcoming my fear and self-consciousness; I had to actually learn *how* to talk with other people.

I carefully watched others to see how they initiated conversations, how they kept them going, and how they ended them. I learned to stop pressuring myself to make witty remarks, to tell dramatic stories, to demonstrate my intelligence. I could be much more at ease, I found, when I was simply sincere. I was most comfortable when I could forget about the words themselves and concentrate on being honest and direct with my feelings.

THOUGHT FOR TODAY: I don't need to be clever. I don't need to be fascinating. I only need to be sincere.

Communication

September 9

Affirmation

I will do all I can to communicate my thoughts and feelings honestly and straightforwardly. I will try to bring the spirit of understanding and love into all I say and the manner in which I say it.

Through positive and caring communications, I will strive for greater closeness in my relationships. I believe that this can best be achieved by reaching out rather than pulling back, and by actively seeking harmony rather than passively remaining on the sidelines.

I will remember that I have nothing to fear from being open and vulnerable. It is then that I can be touched and inspired, that I can feel a true sense of belonging, that I can benefit from shared experiences.

I will be an attentive listener. Listening is a gift of kindness—a way of showing that I care. My goal is to listen compassionately and nonjudgmentally, concentrating on the feelings behind the words.

Through honest and free communication with others, I can be a channel for God's limitless love. By sharing my experience, strength, and hope, I can pass along the gifts that have been generously given to me.

THOUGHT FOR TODAY: The way I communicate can be a manifestation of God's love flowing through me.

37

Self-worth

There is a form of eminence which does not depend on fate; it is an air which sets us apart and seems to portend great things; it is the value which we unconsciously attach to ourselves; it is the quality which wins us the deference of others; more than birth, position or ability, it gives us ascendancy.

—Duc de la Rochefoucauld

September 10

It's always astounding to look back at the trail of devastation caused by our feelings of low self-worth. Those feelings fueled erratic and self-destructive behavior, and propelled us into situations we can't imagine being in today.

As a primary example, we gravitated toward people who were as sick as or sicker than we were. We chose friends or partners who treated us poorly. We tolerated them even when they used and abused us, let us down, or manipulatively "took us" in one way or another.

We thought so little of ourselves that we frequently created or entered precarious situations. We were inclined to take obvious risks, sometimes eagerly so. We drove recklessly, gambled with our health, and occasionally ended up with companions who were dangerous and capable of harming us.

Perhaps worst of all was the mental torture. It was a rare day when we didn't somehow lacerate ourselves with volley after volley of self-deprecation and undeserved criticism.

When we take even a few seconds to remember those thoughts and acts, and how our feelings about ourselves have changed, gratitude comes flooding in. Thank God we don't have to live like that anymore!

THOUGHT FOR TODAY: The war is over. I'm no longer my own worst enemy.

When I was fourteen years old, my mother recounted a vivid dream. I had died, she told me. She and a group of her friends sat around my open coffin in the living room of our home, calmly discussing whether or not I had contributed anything to the world. They concluded that I had not, and therefore, in my mother's words to me, "There was no big loss in your being dead."

It took me a long time to make the connection between such horrendous messages from my parents and the unworthiness I had always felt. My almost complete lack of self-esteem caused me to go through years of self-destructive hell.

The dysfunctional realities in my life eventually brought me to a point of surrender, and a belief that I could be restored by a Power greater than myself. I saw that my life could be turned around; I came to understand that God would guide me and give me strength. But I alone had to be responsible for taking the actions that would override constraining childhood messages, and record freeing new ones.

THOUGHT FOR TODAY: While it is vital to make connections between the past and present, today *I* am responsible for the way I feel about myself.

Self-worth

September 12

Practically every one of us came into recovery with a sense of unworthiness. Some of us had never developed good feelings about ourselves, while others had seen them erode over the years. Therefore, building self-worth became a top priority in our new life.

The problem was, we had no real idea how to begin befriending ourselves. Then it was suggested that the best way to build self-worth was to do worthy things, a day at a time. And that made all the sense in the world.

Day by day, we started taking positive actions that helped us change the way we felt about ourselves. We set out to become rigorously honest, trustworthy, and responsible in all of our affairs. We also committed ourselves to helping others whenever we had the chance.

As time went on, we concentrated on improving our physical, emotional, and spiritual health. We surrounded ourselves with nurturing people, and began to feel deserving of their love and encouragement. We regularly reviewed our progress, and saw that our efforts were paying off. We were indeed developing self-worth a day at a time.

THOUGHT FOR TODAY: By acting in ways that are right and good, I feel right and good about myself.

Our low self-worth caused us to act in ways that camouflaged and distanced us. We would go to virtually any length, albeit unconsciously, to prevent others from seeing what we saw in ourselves. We didn't want anyone to know how inept, inadequate, and unworthy we felt—as far from reality as those feelings may have been.

Perhaps we kept people away by putting on airs of superiority, trying to give the impression that we were in control. Sometimes we erected walls by behaving arrogantly or even outrageously.

Some of us masked our sense of unworthiness by surrounding ourselves with "A-list" people and becoming name-droppers. We pretended that we were "somebody" because we felt we were "nobody." It was also important to appear the best at what we did, even if it was the best of "being bad."

On top of all of that, many of us were driven to acquire various trappings—the "right" clothes, car, or street address—to compensate for our painful feelings about ourselves.

Today, because we've come to know, accept, and love our true selves, we've been able to tear down the walls and discard the masks. We don't need them anymore.

THOUGHT FOR TODAY: Now that I like what I see in myself, I have nothing to hide.

Self-worth

September 14

How do we experience life, now that we have developed self-worth? How does the way we feel about ourselves today compare with the way we used to feel?

When the day begins, we awaken with someone we really care about, rather than despise. That person is ourself.

As we shave or put on makeup, we're able to face the mirror without grimacing. We have positive feelings about how we look, who we are, and what we stand for.

On the way to work we feel capable and confident, rather than fraudulent and anxious. This used to be the worst time of day for us; we projected disastrous scenarios and were consumed with apprehension.

We feel comfortable around other people during the day. We are equal to our fellows, and know that we belong. What a far cry from always feeling like an outsider, alienated and somehow inferior.

At the end of the day we have a sense of fulfillment rather than failure. As sleep overtakes us, we are glad to be alive, and grateful for coming to feel the way we do about ourselves.

THOUGHT FOR TODAY: Now that my inner world has changed, I experience the outer world in an entirely different way.

Self-worth is not something I lacked for years, then suddenly gained, and now have forever. While it's true that I feel good about myself most of the time these days, I've learned not to take those feelings for granted.

The reality is that sometimes my self-worth plummets. On occasion it seems to disappear entirely, if only for a brief interval. When I am sick, for example—even with something as minor as a head cold—I'm extremely vulnerable to my old ideas about myself. At other times, an onslaught of low self-worth can be triggered by a mistake on my part, or someone's thoughtless remark.

When I lapse into my old mind-set and start attacking myself, there are specific restorative actions I can take. Although I can't control the onset of the attack, I can prevent it from escalating into full-scale self-destruction.

Recognizing my negative thoughts for the falsehoods they are, I try to replace them with truth. I share my sense of unworthiness with close friends who remind me that it is part of an old pattern, and offer support. I turn to God, asking Him to help me regain an accurate and honest perception of myself.

THOUGHT FOR TODAY: When feelings of unworthiness temporarily return, I will not despair. I can and will be restored.

Self-worth

September 16

Affirmation

When I look at the person I am today, I appreciate what I see. I accept myself, I care about myself, I value myself.

Because I want to continue feeling this way, I choose to think self-affirming rather than self-deprecating thoughts. I tell myself, "I can do it, I'm capable. I deserve it, I'm worthy."

In the past, the way I felt about myself was determined by the deeds and messages of those around me. Today I know that I alone am responsible for my sense of worth. It's up to me to develop the attitudes and take the actions that will keep me feeling good about myself.

Now that I've come to know and respect my true self, I no longer have to hide behind masks, walls, or possessions. My life decisions—including where to live, what to wear, what to own—are motivated by what is good and right for me, what will make me happy, and what my real needs are.

Self-worth helps me to be comfortable and open around other people, and to be confident in what I do. Especially exciting is the prospect of what I am becoming, and of what still lies ahead.

THOUGHT FOR TODAY: As I heal, I develop an increasing sense of worth from the inside out.

38

Courage

We must have courage to bet on our ideas, to take the calculated risk, and to act. Everyday living requires courage if life is to be effective and bring happiness.

—Maxwell Maltz

September 17

As painful and unacceptable as our lives may have been, for quite some time it seemed easier to let things continue just as they were.

It seemed easier to stay with the familiar—muddling through, barely coping, barely functioning. So we continued to make concessions and compromise our dreams. Year after year, as one example, many of us gave in to the frequently unreasonable or even outrageous demands of parents, partners, or others in our lives.

It seemed easier to continue spiraling downward than to try to do something about our compulsions and addictions. So day after tormenting day, many of us kept on doing the things that made us despise ourselves.

It seemed easier to go on living in quiet desperation than to take the first step and reach out for help.

It took courage—a great deal of courage—to make a commitment to getting well. It took courage to admit the scope of our problems and to surrender. It took courage to listen with an open mind and meet new friends. It took courage to choose a new direction and begin turning our lives around.

THOUGHT FOR TODAY: Recovery *is* the easier, softer way.

During one period of my life, I deluded myself into thinking that certain of my actions were the epitome of courageousness.

Didn't it take courage to get out of a really tight spot by telling a brazenly creative lie with a straight face? Didn't it take guts to pad an expense account or actually steal from an employer without getting caught? And what about escaping from a locked ward—didn't that take a whole lot of courage?

Needless to say, those actions were inspired by recklessness or sheer insanity. They were as far from true courageousness as Earth is from Jupiter.

My perception of courage today is perhaps less dramatic, but definitely more realistic and meaningful. It takes courage, for example, to trust and be guided by a strong inner voice, and to hold fast to one's values. It requires courage to set new goals, to take measured risks, and to follow through with necessary actions a day at a time.

Courage also means being stable, consistent, and responsible in relationships with family and friends. It involves making difficult decisions, and doing what is put in front of us without backing off or running away.

THOUGHT FOR TODAY: Do I sometimes confuse bravado with true courage?

September 19

People sometimes wish it were possible, but no one recovers automatically or by osmosis. We don't get well solely because we've admitted we have a problem, because we've changed our environment, or even because we're associating with other recovering people.

Those of us who were trapped by such thinking got caught in a limbo of sorts. We hovered between our old lives and new ones until we took specific actions to get well.

It required a special kind of courage—and discipline born of that courage—to learn to use and then actually apply the tools that eventually turned our lives around.

When it was time to write a personal inventory to gain self-knowledge, for example, many of us procrastinated. Courage and discipline (among other influences) ultimately made it possible for us to follow through. Similarly, none of us looked forward to disclosing our secrets, past wrongs, and character flaws to another person. But here again, courage gave us the impetus we needed.

To this day it requires a great deal of courage and discipline to make amends, to help others, and to seek God's will—to consistently use all the tools that have already served us well.

THOUGHT FOR TODAY: I have the courage and discipline necessary to practice spiritual principles in all my affairs.

As an outgrowth of my closed-mindedness, I used to feel that certain of my ideas were sacrosanct. I would fight tooth and nail to defend my beliefs about the existence of God, for example, not to mention economic, political, and psychological theories.

One of my most staunchly held views was that I had the power to strongly influence the direction of other people's lives—not only to change them, but to "fix" them if need be. It took years for me to understand that I am powerless in that regard. I have to stand back and let others make their own mistakes and find their own way.

For a long time, I saw myself as a man with "the courage of his convictions." I have since discovered, however, that it usually takes far greater courage to *change* one's convictions than it does to hang on to them.

Surely it takes courage to honestly reevaluate one's views, and to modify or discard them if necessary. And it takes a special kind of courage to do so in a "public" way—to begin developing and living by ideas that may be directly opposite to those that were once vehemently defended.

THOUGHT FOR TODAY: Do I have the courage to change my convictions?

September 21

When we are introduced to a suggested course of action in early recovery, some of us are immediately overwhelmed with fear and self-doubt. All we can think about are past experiences—how we've tried and failed so many times before, in so many ways.

We know in our hearts that it will be impossible to follow through. Even before we start, we're convinced that we just don't have what it takes—courage and discipline.

The truth is, we don't need to have an abundant supply of these qualities when we take our first faltering steps toward getting well. Courage is something that can be acquired over time and through experience. As Ralph Waldo Emerson so aptly put it, "A great part of courage is the courage of having done the thing before."

In that spirit, we acquire courage and develop discipline by walking through our fears a day at a time. Once we've faced a new challenge or tried out an unfamiliar tool the first time, it becomes easier the second time, and easier still the time after that. Before long, what once seemed impossible becomes routine and almost second nature.

THOUGHT FOR TODAY: The courage and discipline I need to meet new challenges can and will be acquired over time.

Some people are of the opinion that spirituality—dependence on God—is a sign of personal weakness. We have come to believe that just the opposite is true, that faith and trust in God is a reflection of one's courage.

Certainly it takes a great deal of courage to admit our powerlessness over other people and many situations. And it takes courage to place our concerns and very destiny in God's hands, acknowledging that where we lack power, He has all power.

To put it another way, it takes considerable courage to make a leap of faith by putting one's life and will in the care of a Higher Power that can't be seen or even defined.

We further believe that faith and trust in God is not only a *reflection* of courage, but also our greatest *source* of courage. Many of us spent years fruitlessly searching for courage in a bottle, in a pill, or in dependence on another person. Today, in faith, we have discovered a reservoir of courage and strength that is inexhaustible and always available to us.

THOUGHT FOR TODAY: I am grateful that it has become possible to replace fear with faith; I am grateful that courage is close at hand.

September 23

Affirmation

I have the courage to do what is necessary to stay on the path of wellness. I have the discipline to seek and do God's will day by day, and to practice spiritual principles in all my affairs. I have the determination to follow the suggestions of my fellows, and to pass along what has been so generously given to me.

I have the courage to look deep within and ask myself, "Where can I change?" I have the willingness to admit and remedy my wrongs, and to disclose and deal with my character flaws.

I have the courage to examine my attitudes and reactions, to abandon my old ideas, and to change my convictions. I have the confidence to be flexible in my relationships with others, to become more open-minded, to adapt to fast-changing environments.

If at times I feel that I lack sufficient courage, I will remind myself that this quality can be acquired over time and through experience. I will remember and be reassured that God is my ultimate source and provider of courage.

THOUGHT FOR TODAY: I have the courage to live a renewed and revitalized life.

39

Forgiveness

The more we know, the better we forgive;
Whoe'er feels deeply, feels for all who live.

—MADAME DE STAËL

September 24

I used to think that forgiveness was an abstract concept that could be practiced only by saints, religious leaders, and the like. When I was hurt or wronged, my natural inclination was always to strike back, to get even, to nurse a grudge. Those of us who were seriously damaged in the past—physically, emotionally, or financially—are especially familiar with such vengeful feelings and acts.

We've since discovered that we too can successfully apply the spiritual principle of forgiveness and, when we do, benefit in very real and practical ways. Forgiveness allows us to deal with our hurt feelings, self-pity, and anger in the best way possible. It prevents these negative emotions from developing into smoldering resentments that can eat away at us for years.

When we forgive someone, it becomes possible to salvage and restore a relationship that otherwise might be destroyed. Moreover, forgiveness allows us to move forward in the present instead of dwelling obsessively in the past.

Many of us believe that the practice of forgiveness brings us closer to God, for we are convinced that He would have us live in this spirit.

THOUGHT FOR TODAY: Forgiveness clears away the negative emotions that cloud our spiritual vision.

For many years the three most frequently used words in my vocabulary were "I," "me," and "hate." I hated my parents for being so hard on me. I hated the army sergeant who made an example of me. I hated the doctor who misdiagnosed me. And so on and so forth.

I was a bitter, resentful person, poisoned by the past and fearful of the future. Because I vehemently resisted forgiving anyone, ever, my hatred owned me.

In my view, forgiveness meant whitewashing wrongs that had been committed. I believed that if I forgave someone, I would condone what they had done and even give up my right to disagree. In short, I would become a doormat.

I eventually reached the point where I could no longer live a life ruled by fear, anger, and hatred. I wanted to change, so much so that I became willing to put aside my pride and at least *try* to be more forgiving.

When I did so, I found that I didn't have to compromise my dignity, sacrifice my principles, or give in to someone else's wrongful behavior. When I began to practice forgiveness, the only thing I gave up was my pain.

THOUGHT FOR TODAY: Forgiveness is neither a concession nor a compromise, but a positive transition to understanding and love.

September 26

We have already made a lot of progress in clearing away the wreckage of the past. Among other actions, we've written and shared a personal inventory, made amends, and released many of our resentments by forgiving the people who harmed us over the years. But what about forgiving *ourselves*?

Even if we have considered self-forgiveness, some of us were unwilling to follow through. We may feel we deserve guilt for our past wrongs; holding on to it is a kind of punishment—a way to keep ourselves under our own thumb. We fail to see that self-forgiveness is as necessary as any other step we've taken to come to terms with the past.

When we finally do forgive ourselves, it can have dramatic and lasting impact on our lives. The memories of our past wrongs are drained of their power to cause us pain. We are able to truly accept the fact that we are no longer the person we used to be, and our self-image can then be revitalized and brought up to date.

THOUGHT FOR TODAY: I, too, deserve forgiveness.

I understood that I had a disease: alcoholism. I also understood that my destructive behavior while drinking was symptomatic of the disease; I was a sick person, not a bad one. And I understood one more thing as well: Unless I forgave myself for the damage I had caused and the wrongs I had done, I could never be entirely free.

Accepting those truths helped me to a degree, but for some reason I couldn't put the whole package together and actually forgive myself.

A month or so later, I heard a man assert, "God loves us unconditionally. No matter what we've done, He will forgive us if we ask Him for forgiveness."

Those words seemed to act as a catalyst, and that very night I prayed for God's forgiveness. I woke up the next morning with this thought in mind: "If God has forgiven me unconditionally—and I know that He has—what right do I have to withhold forgiveness from myself?"

At that point it all came together. I forgave myself, not only for the harm I had caused others, but also for the humiliation, degradation, and destruction I had created in my own life.

THOUGHT FOR TODAY: I can overcome my reluctance to forgive myself by remembering that God has already forgiven me.

September 28

"The other night I heard someone go on and on about how she couldn't stand to be around her father, and I could really relate to that," my friend said to me. "For most of my life I had that same kind of feeling. I hated both of my parents with a passion.

"When they died I thought I would feel differently," she continued, "but even after a year I still had tremendous anger and bitterness toward them. Only it was worse, because I also felt guilty.

"By then all that turmoil inside of me was spilling over into every part of my life. I had to get rid of those unresolved feelings, I knew I did. One of the things that helped me most was to forgive my parents, even though they were dead.

"When someone first made that suggestion, it seemed really pointless," she added. "But I did it anyway. Soon I began to feel better inside, and I actually started thinking good things about my mother and father instead of all that usual garbage. That's when I understood why I needed to forgive them. I had to do it for one reason alone—for *my* sake—for my sanity and peace of mind."

THOUGHT FOR TODAY: Remember the healing power of forgiveness.

When we first tapped into the power of forgiveness, we saw its value in only limited ways. Certainly it helped us get over our hurt feelings, kept us from developing resentments, and brought us back to a peaceful frame of mind. In short, forgiveness did what we had been promised it would.

We have since come to know a lot more about forgiveness. We see it not simply as an isolated act taken to achieve a specific purpose, but as a new consciousness of sorts—a spiritual approach to living that allows us to coexist peacefully with everything and everyone.

When we live in a spirit of forgiveness, it becomes possible to recognize ourselves in people who have harmed us—and to acknowledge that we are capable of committing the very same wrongs. We can more easily understand that such people may be spiritually or emotionally off balance, that they are doing the best they can based on the circumstances of their life experiences.

As forgiving people, we offer not only pardon to those who wrong us, but also kindness, compassion, and generosity of spirit.

THOUGHT FOR TODAY: I will try to live in the spirit of forgiveness.

September 30

Affirmation

I believe in my heart that God has forgiven me, and that He will do so again and again whenever I ask Him. In this same spirit, I try to forgive myself, as well as others who have harmed me.

The thread that runs through my relationships today is one of love rather than hatred. This is so because I strive to be a forgiving person, and no longer collect and store wrongs that have been committed against me.

I've come to see that forgiveness is not a concession or compromise, as I once thought, but a positive act involving such character traits as understanding, compassion, and kindness. Even more important is the realization that I practice forgiveness more for my own sake than the sake of others.

I'm grateful that I have finally forgiven myself. I no longer need to use guilt as self-punishment, and my past acts have been drained of their power to hurt me. Because of self-forgiveness, I have stopped seeing myself as the person I used to be, and can now accept myself as the person I have become.

THOUGHT FOR TODAY: As I forgive myself and others who have hurt me, I experience a new dimension of freedom.

40

Freedom

To have freedom is only to have that which is absolutely necessary to enable us to be what we ought to be, and to possess what we ought to possess.

—I. RAHEL

October 1

When I think about the destructive power of my addictions and obsessions, this scene from a movie sometimes comes to mind: A man is trapped in a small room with no exit; the walls, which are studded with sharp spikes, are inching ever closer . . . .

For half my life I was a prisoner of alcoholism. As my disease progressed, my cell grew smaller, and my awareness of the outside world diminished. I all but missed two decades of social, economic, and political change. Each year, my circle of friends and possible rescuers grew smaller.

At the end, my every thought centered around drinking—getting through a hangover, getting out of trouble, getting money to drink some more.

My world has opened wide since then, but it quickly closes in again when I become obsessed with something. I lose the freedom to think about anything else, to look elsewhere, to move about.

When an obsession begins to take hold, I try not to waste time willing or wishing it away. I turn to God, to the power that freed me from the confinement of my addictions. He restores me to sanity and gives me back my freedom.

THOUGHT FOR TODAY: When I become obsessed, I lose my freedom.

More often than not, we blamed others for our lack of personal freedom. We thought, "If only he would stop needing me so much . . ." "If only she would let me do what I want . . ." "If only they would leave me alone . . ."

Ultimately, we had to admit that the restrictions and emotional burdens placed on us by others were far less confining than those we placed on ourselves. It was our preoccupation with self that kept us in bondage.

Because of our drive for perfection, for example, we set unattainable goals and remained in servitude to them; even when we completed a task, we couldn't be free of it. Moreover, our painful self-consciousness often prevented us from seeing things accurately, from thinking clearly and acting spontaneously. Perhaps the most unyielding restraint of all was the way we obsessively focused on our every desire, feeling, symptom, scheme.

We found freedom from the bondage of self through spiritual growth. Our limited objectives began to mean less and less to us, while God's will began to mean more and more. We began to understand that we could be far happier by serving others—and thus serving God—than by thinking only of ourselves.

THOUGHT FOR TODAY: By moving toward spiritual objectives, I become free of the bondage of self.

October 3

As part of my recovery program, it was suggested that I unflinchingly review my past and present relationships. That way, I was told, I could learn a great deal about the structure and strictures of my interactions with others, and avoid making the same mistakes again.

When I looked with new eyes and an open mind, clear patterns emerged. I could see that many of my relationships had never been free.

In some cases, I "took hostages" instead of having friendships. That is to say, I had the egocentric idea that others were put in my path to serve me. I was demanding and controlling, and insisted on absolute loyalty. At other times, *I* became an all-too-willing hostage by abdicating my freedom to someone else.

I understand today that the healthiest relationships are those in which great respect is given to individual freedom: The freedom to be oneself, without feeling the necessity to change for another person. The freedom to have aspirations, to make one's own decisions and mistakes. The freedom to be honest and forthright without fear of reprisal. The freedom to grow emotionally and spiritually at one's own pace.

THOUGHT FOR TODAY: Do I fully respect the personal freedom of my friends and loved ones?

Freedom   316

For all intents and purposes, we were adults. We were living on our own and self-supporting. We voted in elections, paid taxes, and in some cases were married and had children of our own.

Yet even with all the credentials of maturity, we had never become completely free to think and act as adults. All too often, we were more responsive to the whims and wishes of our parents than to our own feelings and needs. All too often, we reverted to a childlike need for approval, and made gut-wrenching concessions to get it.

Thankfully, with a lot of courage and hard work, along with the support of friends and a loving God, we were finally able to break free.

Today, we no longer feel compelled to live up to our parents' expectations. We no longer accept guilt when it is delivered. We are free of the fear of emotional abuse; our parents may still be serving it up, but we no longer take it to heart or respond in kind.

Most important, we are able to live healthy and unfettered lives—and we are able to pass that same health and freedom on to future generations.

THOUGHT FOR TODAY: Adulthood doesn't guarantee a release from my past patterns. I will take the initiative to break free.

October 5

For years we had hoped for it, prayed for it, fantasized about it. And then it finally happened: we were free at last.

Some of us ended destructive relationships in which we had been emotionally drained. Some of us moved out of dysfunctional homes where we had been stifled. Some of us escaped from jobs where we had been taken for granted and demeaned.

It soon turned out, however, that our freedom was an illusion. We were already involved with someone just as abusive and draining as our parents or former partner. We were already in a new job even more demeaning and devaluing of our talents than the one we had fought so hard to leave.

We were unaware that we were doing so, yet we sought out and settled into situations and relationships almost identical to the ones we had before.

When we finally dug deeply enough to find out why we still weren't free, this is what we discovered: All that had really changed in our lives were the settings and circumstances. We ourselves hadn't changed enough on the inside to obtain true and lasting personal freedom.

THOUGHT FOR TODAY: Just because we think we've escaped, that doesn't mean we're free.

Sometimes when I wake up in the morning I try to lie quietly for a while, thinking about some of the things in my life for which I'm grateful. Freedom from fear, freedom from the past, freedom from addiction—these are the obvious gifts that come quickly to mind.

Occasionally, I end up thinking about a less obvious freedom: freedom of the spirit. Perhaps ironically, the free-spiritedness that has come to mean so much to me today is a quality I never knew I lacked.

My free spirit encourages me to expand my consciousness, to explore new ways of doing things, to set new goals. I'm not bound by old ideas that once narrowed my perspective and kept me trapped on a treadmill of despair.

My free spirit tells me that I can be an individual, that I don't have to conform, that the limitations of others need not be my limitations. I'm not inhibited by societal pressures.

My free spirit opens my eyes and mind to limitless new choices and opportunities. Life for me is no longer a one-horse race around a muddy track.

THOUGHT FOR TODAY: Freedom begins within me.

October 7

Affirmation

My world is wide and I am free. So long as I practice spiritual principles, my freedom will increase. So long as I am willing to forgive, to accept, and to change within, I will remain free.

I am free to live comfortably and with positive purpose in the here and now. I have come to terms with my life as it once was. I have left behind guilt, destructive behavior, and other constraints of the past.

There is increasing freedom and satisfaction in my relationships. They are no longer hobbled by a need on my part for complete agreement, loyalty, or control. Instead, my goal is to be respectful and supportive of the needs and aspirations of others.

I am finding freedom from the bondage of self. I no longer am limited by self-centered thoughts, emotions, and drives. My attention has shifted to the present moment. I have a growing concern for my fellows and the will of God.

I have freedom of the spirit. I am not restricted by outdated views and goals. I am free to explore new ways of doing things, and to seek out new options and opportunities.

THOUGHT FOR TODAY: My God-given freedoms are unconditional, and apply to all areas of my life.

Freedom   320

41

Service to Others

*I expect to pass through life but once. If, therefore
there can be any kindness I can show, or any good
thing I can do to any fellow being, let me do it now,
and not defer or neglect it, as I shall not pass this way
again.*

—WILLIAM PENN

October 8

We used to think that the whole point of life was to get as much as you could, and hang on to it at all costs. It seemed crystal clear: The more you give away, the less you have for yourself.

If we were willing to give at all, we did so selectively, with the idea that some people were more worthy than others of whatever it was we chose to give.

The end result of that way of life was not personal enrichment, as we had expected, but a pervasive sense of emptiness. It led us to sometimes ask such plaintive questions as, "Why am I here? What's the point of all this?"

Many of us found answers to those seemingly unanswerable questions when we began to follow a spiritual path. Our purpose in life, we've come to believe, is to serve God. And we further believe that He would have us do so by serving others.

This is what gives us a true sense of usefulness and fulfillment today. We have learned that giving of ourselves enhances rather than diminishes us. Even as we give, we receive—and the more we give, the more we receive.

THOUGHT FOR TODAY: Service to others brings purpose and enrichment to my life.

I was going through one of those periods when it seemed that the bottom was falling out of everything. After several weeks of anguish, I called a friend. He listened patiently while I whined and complained. Then he made two specific suggestions.

The first was to "pray for knowledge of God's will and the power to carry it out," and the second was to "find somebody worse off than you are, and try to help them."

I was annoyed at the suggestions, because obviously they had nothing to do with my problems. Soon, however, the problems worsened, so in desperation I took my friend's advice.

I prayed as he had suggested. Then, when the opportunity presented itself, I found myself reaching out to a newly sober alcoholic by sharing my own "before-and-after" story.

What happened after I took these actions may have been predictable to my friend, but it was revelationary to me. Everything improved.

For one thing, my actions took me out of myself. For another, the problems were reduced to their right size, and I regained perspective. Finally, by turning to God and reaching out to another person, I was reminded of what's really important in life.

THOUGHT FOR TODAY: One of the best ways to help myself is by helping someone else.

Service to Others

October 10

It's easy to know what to do when a friend or loved one needs a place to stay, an emergency loan, or moral support during a hospital stay or similar crisis. But how can we help others when such opportunities don't present themselves? And how can we be generous of spirit to people beyond our immediate circle?

Each day, wherever we go, there are countless opportunities to be of service. Certainly we can be friendly and considerate to anyone who crosses our path. And we can always reach out in a special way to another person, even a stranger, by listening attentively and showing interest in what they have to say.

Moreover, we can let people know we are available if they need us. We can pass along compliments, and offer encouragement and approval. Sometimes, simple courtesy or a warm smile can be as welcome as a far more dramatic action.

When we are new at reaching out to others, we may have to consciously look for opportunities to do so. Before long, though—because we gain so much from it—service to others becomes second nature to us.

THOUGHT FOR TODAY: If I'm willing to be there for others, the opportunities will be there for me.

A friend of mine swims daily in a pool located on a nearby college campus. Several weeks after a new man had been hired to clean and maintain the pool, my friend noticed a huge difference.

"For the first time in a long time, the pool was being kept spotless," she told me. "One day, on an impulse, I called up the athletic director to let him know what a good job the new man was doing."

Her call, brief as it was, evoked an unexpected reaction. The athletic director was flabbergasted that someone had actually taken the time to express appreciation for a job well done.

"His reaction made me aware again of what happens in my life when I reach out. By helping someone else, even in a small or indirect way, I help myself. I feel good, and useful. Also, when I'm thinking about others, and doing for them, I know I'm on the right track as far as my emotional health and stability are concerned.

"The other thing is," she added, "when I reach out—whether it's impulsively, like that phone call, or something I've planned—it always makes me feel closer to God."

THOUGHT FOR TODAY: I will take the time and make the effort to reach out to others.

October 12

We are deeply grateful that our lives have been transformed. We are thankful to a loving God, and to the people He has brought into our lives to show us the way.

The most satisfying and meaningful way to express gratitude for what we have been given— experience, strength, and hope—is to pass along those same gifts to others. In doing so, we find that the benefits of service go far beyond feeling good and being able to show appreciation.

When we reach out to another person and share what we have learned about getting well, it keeps us involved in the healing process. Often, what we say to someone else is exactly what we need to hear again ourselves. We are reminded of the principles that changed our lives—in particular, learning to trust God, and to live one day at a time.

By helping others get through their pain and confusion, we are also sharply reminded of how we used to feel. And those reminders play a key role in preventing us from slipping back into our old ways of thinking and acting.

THOUGHT FOR TODAY: In order to keep the gifts of experience, strength, and hope, I will pass them on to others.

There was a time in my life when self-sufficiency was my byword. Whenever anyone offered to help me, my immediate and almost violent reaction was, "I can handle it by myself—just leave me alone!"

Frequently, the help that was offered could have meant a lot. It could have saved me time, money, and grief. Nevertheless, in those days it was simply impossible for me to accept help in the spirit in which it was intended. The way I saw it, if someone offered help, it meant one of two things: Either they thought I was incapable, or they wanted something from me.

Besides a lack of trust, my considerable pride wouldn't allow me to appear "needy." Something in my upbringing made it necessary to constantly prove myself through my alleged accomplishments and seeming independence.

Perhaps most significant, my low self-worth told me I had no right to anyone's help, because I didn't deserve it.

In my case, learning how to accept help was just as important as learning how to be helpful. It has taken time, willingness, and the patience of others for me to be able to let people in.

THOUGHT FOR TODAY: When help is offered, I will try to accept it graciously and trustingly.

Affirmation

Service to others has become an indispensable part of my new life. By serving my fellows, I also serve God, and at the same time gain a true sense of usefulness and fulfillment. The more I give of myself, the more I receive.

Today I will try to be aware of opportunities to serve others. I will reach out in subtle ways as well as obvious ones by being friendly, attentive, and considerate. When I think about others and am willing to do what I can for them, it is a sure sign that I am making progress in my recovery.

If I become immersed in my problems to the point of preoccupation, I can always help myself by helping someone else. Reaching out to others reduces my self-involvement, and allows me to regain perspective.

God has brought others into my life to show me the way, and it is now incumbent upon me to share the experience, strength, and hope that have been so freely given. Through my actions, I can remain involved in the healing process, and express my gratitude to God for all my blessings.

THOUGHT FOR TODAY: I will stand in readiness to be of service to others.

42

Living in the Now

The only use of a knowledge of the past is to equip us for the present. No more deadly harm can be done to young minds than by depreciation of the present. The present contains all that there is. It is holy ground; for it is the past, and it is the future.

—ALFRED NORTH WHITEHEAD

October 15

Like so many people, I spent a lot of time living in the future or past, instead of the present. In my mind, I created elaborate, fear-generated scenarios about events that might occur. I also constantly rehashed mistakes, missed opportunities, and wrongs committed against me.

Certain well-used phrases reflected my preoccupation with yesterday and tomorrow. Future-related phrases were along the lines of "What if . . . ?" "Suppose . . . ," and "I hope . . . ." Examples: "What if I can't make next year's payments?" "What if I have to have surgery?"

Similarly, past-related phrases included "I should have . . . ," and "I can't believe I . . . ." Examples: "I should have gotten even." "I can't believe I accepted their first offer."

I've come to realize that fearful projection about tomorrow or guilty regrets about yesterday are opposite sides of the same self-destructive coin.

When I slip back into using such cautionary or admonishing phrases, I try to recognize that I'm causing myself needless stress and worry. If I can do that, it then becomes relatively easy to put aside concerns about the past and future, and come back to the present moment.

THOUGHT FOR TODAY: Projection, either forward or backward, shatters my peace of mind and deprives me of the present moment.

There once was a child whose life was filled with fear and uncertainty. Whenever his alcoholic parents got drunk and became violent, he hid in his bedroom closet until the turmoil subsided.

In the darkness, the child escaped into a world of fantasy. Most often, he either pressed a vein on his wrist to become invisible, or entered a space capsule that would render him invulnerable and take him anywhere in the universe.

As the child grew into adulthood, he continued to escape from unpleasant realities. Although he no longer relied on comic-book fantasies to get him through, he found other, more acceptable ways to isolate and insulate himself. He often put in fourteen-hour days at work, or found solace in overeating.

Just after his thirty-fifth birthday, it dawned on him that his ongoing escapes were keeping him trapped in the bedroom closet of his past. He realized that he wasn't really growing or getting anywhere, and that nothing would ever change unless he began dealing with his feelings, fears, and pain.

It was time to stop running away, he saw, and to start living in the here and now.

THOUGHT FOR TODAY: Am I allowing myself to grow emotionally—or am I still seeking ways to escape into my "bedroom closet"?

October 17

For long stretches of time, we sat on the side-lines of life. We were so caught up in fear, projection, and unresolved conflicts that it was impossible to actively participate in the present moment.

Today we have a zest for living. We insist on *experiencing* life rather than taking it for granted or letting it pass us by. We are determined to use our minds and bodies—each of our miraculous senses—to the fullest. Therefore, one of our overriding goals is to stay in the now.

Depending on what is going on in our lives, this can frequently be a formidable undertaking. Nevertheless, we try the very best we can to concentrate on what's actually occurring, as well as how we experience and respond to it.

Life means the most when we assimilate what is taking place around us—when we feel our feelings. So we do our utmost to be physically and emotionally present as each moment unfolds.

We don't let worry about the future keep us from appreciating a present blessing. Nor do we allow the memory of past pain to shut out the sound and joy of today's laughter.

THOUGHT FOR TODAY: Yesterday is history, tomorrow is a mystery.

I remember the first time that someone suggested I live my life "a day at a time." She presented the idea as if imparting a priceless nugget of wisdom. I smiled to myself and shrugged inwardly. "What's the big deal about that?" I thought. "How else does one live, if not a day at a time?"

Before long, however, my closed-minded and know-it-all attitude changed radically. She was absolutely right, I saw. There was indeed great wisdom in the suggestion that I live a day at a time.

Hadn't I always approached new challenges in their entirety, as something to be taken on all at once? Hadn't I been frustrated countless times by my unrealistic expectations? Hadn't I frequently been overwhelmed by what I faced or might face in the weeks, months, or years ahead?

I've since learned that I can reduce even the most formidable task to manageability by approaching it a day at a time—or, if that's too much, an hour or even five minutes at a time. I've discovered, moreover, that I can successfully accomplish and get through just about anything—from routine responsibilities to an unexpected trauma—a day at a time.

THOUGHT FOR TODAY: Am I still taking on everything all at once—or am I learning to live one day at a time?

October 19

We were intrigued by the new friends we met in recovery. They were vital and friendly; they appeared to be comfortable in their surroundings and with themselves. They also seemed to know what they were doing, and where they were headed in life.

There was no question about it: We wanted what they had, and we wanted it right away. So we began pressuring ourselves to get well all at once.

Needless to say, that's not how recovery takes place. We find our way back just as we lost our way—one day at a time. We recover gradually, growing not only through enlightenment and joy, but also through challenges and pain.

The character defects we've struggled with for years don't suddenly vanish overnight. Our lifelong attitude of negativity can't be reversed in a few short weeks. Careers and relationships can't be rebuilt without a great deal of time and effort.

In short, every area of our life can and will change—but only a day at a time. So we need to be patient and understanding with ourselves, remembering that we can only do the best we can—*today*.

THOUGHT FOR TODAY: Each day brings new opportunities to grow and change.

"If you must project, why not project positively?" people sometimes said. "Why not project good things for yourself, instead of only disaster?"

At first, this suggestion made a lot of sense. It seemed to work. Before long, though, some of us found that positive projection could cause us just as much trouble as negative projection.

For one thing, when we projected "positively" into the future, it was hard not to *depend* on our wishes coming true. For another, we tended to get carried away; we developed unrealistic expectations and, more often than not, set ourselves up for major disappointments.

And there was yet another problem. When we projected positively, the exact same thing happened as when we projected negatively: We left the present moment and departed from reality.

Since we are human, it's virtually impossible to avoid projection entirely. There is one thing, however, that can do wonders in helping us stay in the now. We can focus on God, and His will for good in our lives. Because we trust Him, we know that whatever the future brings will be ultimately beneficial. That knowledge, deep and unshakeable within us, can make it far easier to live in and enjoy the present moment.

THOUGHT FOR TODAY: When I'm close to God, I'm less inclined to wonder and worry about the future.

Living in the Now

October 21

Affirmation

I choose to live my life in the here and now. I am willing and able to deal with all of life's issues and to feel all of my feelings, not only the ones I find pleasant and acceptable. There may be some pain, but there surely will be much joy.

I choose to stay in the present moment, rather than concern myself with yesterday or tomorrow. I can make use of the past, and I can look forward to the future, but I exist and flourish in the present.

I choose to enhance my life rather than try to escape from it. Each day brings me new opportunities to discover more about myself, to overcome my character flaws, to improve my relationships, and to strengthen my bond with God. However, I will not pressure myself to achieve any of these objectives all at once.

I remind myself that I don't have to take on anything in its entirety. By staying in the now and living my life a day at a time, I can successfully meet any challenge and make the most of every opportunity.

THOUGHT FOR TODAY: If not here, where? If not now, when?

43

Priorities

No horse gets anywhere till he is harnessed. No steam or gas ever drives anything until it is confined. No Niagara is ever turned into light and power until it is tunneled. No life ever grows great until it is focused, dedicated, disciplined.

—HARRY EMERSON FOSDICK

October 22

We have worked diligently to develop positive values and a praiseworthy code of behavior. As the result, we feel better about ourselves than we ever have. So we're not about to let anyone or anything chip away at our hard-won personal integrity.

On a day-to-day basis, this means staying committed to self-honesty and self-restraint. When we are at work, for example, we do our best to maintain our standards and uphold our ideals, even though we could get by with less. Or if someone we're close to goes on an emotional rampage and tries to take things out on us, we don't sink to his or her level by retaliating in kind. In short, we don't cut corners in any area of our lives.

Maintaining personal integrity remains high on our list of priorities because it helps us build self-esteem. Each time we stand by our principles, we're rewarded with good feelings about ourselves. Besides that, we no longer can get away with those "little compromises" in our attitudes and actions. The price is too high, and we refuse to pay it.

THOUGHT FOR TODAY: My willingness to uphold my values is a clear indication of how I value myself.

Spirituality meant absolutely nothing to me when I entered recovery. My attitude was, "If you believe in that sort of thing, fine; just leave me out of it."

Over a period of time, I gradually became more open-minded about faith—by observing its dynamics in the lives of others, and by tentatively testing it myself. My faith grew, but for several years it was no more than an adjunct to my life, ranked just below family and career.

Yet I progressed spiritually in spite of myself. And the more I progressed, the more purpose, fulfillment, and satisfaction there was in my life. That's why I ultimately made spiritual growth a top priority.

Today, spirituality is the very hub of my existence, from which all else radiates. Whenever there is a problem in any area of my life, I can rely on spiritual tools to provide a solution. No matter what takes place, I can find stability and serenity by returning to my spiritual center.

I strongly believe that there is an opportunity for spiritual growth for me in all of life's experiences—in every dilemma or disappointment, every detour or rough spot, every success or seeming failure.

THOUGHT FOR TODAY: Spiritual growth is a priority, but it is also more than that. It gives my life meaning and purpose.

October 24

We all know people who zealously put everyone else ahead of themselves on their list of priorities. Some of us also were like that. We worried so much about others that we neglected to care for ourselves.

We were so obsessed with the destructive behavior and unending problems of our loved ones and friends, that we were blind to our own behavior and problems. For years we willingly took responsibility for everyone and everything around us, but failed to take responsibility for ourselves.

For those of us who fell into this trap of codependence, recovery has meant, as much as anything else, a rearrangement of priorities.

We've had to realize that we can't solve problems that are not our own, that we are not responsible for other people's behavior. We've had to learn that so long as we insist on controlling and managing the lives of others, our own lives will be out of control and unmanageable.

Our priority today is to put ourselves first, even when we sometimes feel undeserving. That means being aware and responsible for our feelings and actions, living our own lives, and being caring and considerate of ourselves.

THOUGHT FOR TODAY: My responsibility is to myself; I can't force wellness on others.

Before recovery, I rarely thought about my behavior or looked at the motives behind it. I did what I thought I had to do to get by; I acted on whim, impulse, or pure reflex.

If I did briefly search out the motives for a particular action, I usually deluded myself in some way. When I spent money on others, for example, I often conned myself into believing I was doing so out of generosity. My real motive, however, was to gain approval or buy favors. When I was sarcastic and teasing, I believed that I was being humorous; my real motive was to send out a verbal jab and "get" someone.

Today, in sharp contrast, an important priority is to examine my motives before I act. I try to make certain that I am doing the right thing for the right reasons; that way, I can change my course of action if need be.

By staying aware of my motives, I can avoid being hurtful to others, and prevent myself from doing something I may later regret. I can also learn more about myself, especially when those same ill-advised motives surface repeatedly.

THOUGHT FOR TODAY: It takes but a few seconds to check my motives, to ask "Why am I doing this?"

October 26

When I had intuitive feelings in the past, they were frequently drowned out by more demanding emotions, including rage or dread. At other times I relied so heavily on my intellect when making decisions that I was completely out of touch with my gut feelings.

For the most part, however, I simply refused to listen; experience had taught me that to trust my intuition was to court disaster. (In this latter instance, what I thought was intuition was in reality self-delusion or self-will running riot.)

My inner voice has since taken on greater authority and new importance. These days, I listen for it, and almost always heed its urgings. In fact, when my mind tells me one thing and my inner voice suggests something else, I am inclined to go along with the intuitive feeling. For I know now that it speaks truth and will likely guide me in the right direction.

Over the years, I have become convinced that at times my inner voice is an expression of God's will for me. As my faith and trust in Him—and in myself—grows stronger, my inner voice becomes more distinct.

THOUGHT FOR TODAY: My inner voice is a valuable asset, and I will treat it accordingly.

We thought it sounded a bit fanatical when we were told that our physical and emotional sobriety must come before anyone or anything else. But now we understand. Sobriety must indeed be our number one priority, because without it we have nothing.

Our own painful experience has taught us that the minute we begin taking our sobriety for granted, it will begin to slip away. If we don't quickly get our priorities back in order, we are bound to become as physically, mentally, and spiritually bankrupt as we once were.

To be more specific, if a relationship is causing unrelenting pain and turmoil for us, we may have to consider ending it. Similarly, the job we have may be a "plum," but it's not for us if it causes undue stress in our life and impinges on our recovery needs.

Today we put first things first. We try to have an unequivocal willingness to do whatever is necessary to maintain our physical and emotional well-being. No job, no relationship, no amount of money or status is worth our sobriety.

THOUGHT FOR TODAY: Are my priorities in order? Do I truly believe that sobriety must come first, no matter what?

Priorities

October 28

Affirmation

My priorities have changed dramatically and, consequently, so has the quality of my life. Where once I devoted my entire attention to the outer world—clamoring for ever more approval, love, and gratification—today I concentrate on nurturing and expanding my inner self.

First and foremost, I have the willingness to do whatever is necessary to maintain my physical and emotional sobriety. To lose sight of this priority would be to jeopardize all I have worked for and all I have gained.

Personal integrity also is of paramount importance. This is because my self-esteem grows each time I uphold my values, speak my mind, evaluate my motives, and do the right things for the right reasons.

Spirituality, too, ranks high as a priority, but it has become more than that—it has become the very core of my being. So long as I remain open-minded, rely on spiritual principles, practice prayer and meditation, and learn from my experiences, I will continue to grow spiritually. And so long as I grow spiritually, the quality of my life will continue to improve—of that I am certain.

THOUGHT FOR TODAY: I will not lose sight of my priorities, for they are the guideposts of progress.

44

Humility

Humility is not a weak and timid quality; it must be carefully distinguished from a groveling spirit. There is such a thing as an honest pride and self-respect. Though we may be servants of all, we should be servile to none.

—EDWIN HUBBELL CHAPIN

October 29

If people we knew were conceited and egotistical, it was apparent to us that they "had no humility." That's as far as our understanding of humility went. When we set out on a spiritual path and explored this trait in depth, we saw that it could literally transform our lives, by freeing us from the bondage of self.

To get a real grasp of humility, we first examined its opposite: pride. Of all our character defects, it was perhaps the most damaging. Because of pride, we were propelled by willfulness, convinced that dogged self-reliance was the best way to get through life. As the result of this kind of self-reliance, we dug ourselves into a deep hole; the harder we tried to get out on our own, the further we fell.

Humility, in sharp contrast, provides us with a true estimate of ourselves—our weaknesses as well as our strengths. It allows us to accept our personal limitations and our powerlessness over people, places, and things.

We've come to understand humility as the pursuit of spiritual rather than material objectives. Our continuing goal is to give up self-will in order to seek and do God's will.

THOUGHT FOR TODAY: Pride binds me to myself; humility brings me closer to God.

Three or four years into my recovery, I was grappling unsuccessfully with a career problem. When I talked about it at length with a friend, he suggested that I needed to gain more humility. I was quite surprised at his advice. In fact, I was insulted.

At the time, I thought humility meant being humbled in some negative way. And I'd already had more than enough of *that*. As a child, I had been emotionally abused; over the years I had been criticized, degraded, and shot down more times than I cared to remember. So if anybody had humility, I did.

My friend explained that humility had nothing to do with *humiliation*, nor did one gain it by self-abasement. "To me," he said, "humility has to do with myself in relation to God. It means I have only limited power to change myself and the world around me, and that He has all power to do so.

"When I approach a problem with humility," he added pointedly, "I don't spend as much time butting my head against the wall, trying to figure things out on my own. In other words, humility means accepting my limitations, and then asking for God's help and guidance."

THOUGHT FOR TODAY: Humility enhances rather than diminishes my capabilities.

October 31

We had been driven to our knees by addictions and compulsions, tied in knots by the emotional scars of childhood. We had been shattered by grief over the loss of someone very dear.

The causes of our anguish may have differed, but the results were the same: All of us eventually conceded our powerlessness over the way we were feeling and acting.

In our desperation, we turned to God for help. He did for us what we could not do for ourselves. Our addictions and obsessions were removed; our grief and pain were assuaged.

Later, a remarkable new possibility was presented to us: If God's power could relieve us of lifelong compulsions and see us through calamities, why couldn't that same power be applied in other areas of our lives? Why couldn't we ask God to free us from our anger, impatience, fear, and intolerance—those lingering personality flaws we'd never been able to get rid of on our own?

When we were completely ready and willing to give up those damaging character traits, we put our faith in God's power. He was there for us, as He always has been, as He always will be.

THOUGHT FOR TODAY: When I humbly turn to Him, God always responds.

When we were finally willing to have our short-comings removed and humbly turned to God, they *were* removed—sometimes all at once, sometimes gradually. For many of us, this was the first time we had tested our faith; we were amazed and delighted with the results. We knew with certainty we had a faith that worked.

But there was more to it than that. Since we're human, we're sometimes inclined to revitalize a character defect when we sense it might be useful. We throw a tantrum, for example, to get our way. We may also temporarily try to run the show, forgetting how powerless we really are.

In spite of our occasional excursions into willfulness, we believe that God always stands ready to exert His power on our behalf, so long as we humbly ask Him to do so.

We also believe that we must do our part—the "footwork"—in order to show our willingness. We may ask God to remove our impatience, selfishness, or explosive temper, for example. But we also need to act in faith by trying to be as patient and unselfish as we can, and by exercising self-restraint to the best of our ability.

THOUGHT FOR TODAY: God's strength is always available, even when I "take back" my will or try to exhume an old behavior.

November 2

Through my own experience and that of my friends, I've found that humility isn't a concept with clear boundaries. It means different things to different people.

Some define humility as a willingness to acknowledge one's shortcomings and limitations. Others see it as a true recognition of who we really are, followed by an honest attempt to become what we could be. Still others describe humility as a desire to seek and do God's will.

Each of these definitions makes sense, but I've also come to understand and appreciate humility on a far more personal basis in my life.

When I *lack* humility, all I can think about is how I look, how I feel, how I measure up, what I want, what I should get, and what I might lose. I worry about yesterday and am fearful about tomorrow. I experience frustration, anxiety, and irritability.

When I have humility, on the other hand, I think less about myself and more about others and God. I feel serene and truly free. I know that fundamentally all is well, and that God will see me through any difficulties I may have.

THOUGHT FOR TODAY: God is in charge, and His plan for good in my life is on schedule.

We have finally begun to have a clear understanding of humility—of how it takes us out of ourselves and brings us closer to God. We see that it is a character trait worth acquiring, and we want to do just that.

But humility can also seem to be a lofty and almost abstract spiritual goal, a private and even mysterious interaction between ourselves and God. It wasn't very difficult figuring out how to apply various other spiritual principles—such as kindness and honesty—in everyday life. Humility, however, can seem almost "too spiritual" in a dog-eat-dog world.

But that isn't the case at all, we realize after a while. There are actions and attitudes of all kinds that can help us acquire humility on a day-to-day basis.

Now we can back off after taking something as far as possible. We can admit our mistakes, learn to say "I don't know," ask questions, and show respect for other people's experience and knowledge.

In addition, we can see ourselves as equals and treat others as we would be treated. And we can try to be accepting and grateful for what God has given to us.

THOUGHT FOR TODAY: I can acquire humility through one act at a time, one thought at a time, one day at a time.

November 4

Affirmation

Humility is a lifetime undertaking. Years upon years of self-centeredness cannot be overcome all at once. So I will strive each day to keep myself right-size and in perspective, remembering that I have only limited power, while God has all power.

I will endeavor to put spiritual values foremost among my priorities, for I have come to understand that material satisfactions by themselves can never bring lasting peace of mind. Neither can they bring a true sense of purpose and usefulness to my life.

I once believed that humility stood apart from other spiritual qualities—that one could acquire it only through great pain and suffering, or by becoming "saintly" in some way. I have since learned that I can gain humility a day at a time, by taking specific actions to become free of self.

I will try to put God first. In spite of my periodic detours into willfulness, I believe that His love for me is unwavering. So long as I approach Him with humility, His help will always be forthcoming.

THOUGHT FOR TODAY: Humility is no longer something I *must* have, but something I truly want.

45

Self-assertion

Be noble-minded! Our own heart, and not other men's opinions of us, forms our true honor.

—JOHANN CHRISTOPH FRIEDRICH VON SCHILLER

November 5

Like so many people, I developed the conviction growing up that my feelings, ideas, and opinions were unimportant. Consequently, I rarely expressed my views, even when I felt strongly about something. In order to blend in and hide my sense of insignificance, I tailored my opinions and actions to what others said and did.

Even as an adult, I frequently behaved as I thought you wanted me to behave. I would root for your team, side with you against your wife or husband, and give you moral support even when you were clearly in the wrong.

My chameleonlike behavior grew out of (and perpetuated) deep feelings of inferiority that told me I wasn't smart enough, capable enough, creative enough, or worthy enough.

One of my primary challenges in recovery has been to develop as an individual in my own right. I've had to discover who I really am, and what I really believe and feel—regardless of the influences of others.

A parallel challenge has been to develop the kind of self-worth that makes it possible not only to express my true beliefs and opinions, but to stand behind them as well.

THOUGHT FOR TODAY: If it's important to speak up, I'll do so—even when I'm tempted to passively "blend in."

Self-assertion 354

If we grew up in dysfunctional homes where turmoil and trauma were everyday realities, we did our best to stay out of the line of fire. We kept our mouths shut and our feelings to ourselves; we almost always backed down in order to keep the peace, no matter how strongly we felt about something. We learned to say "yes" with a straight face even when our hearts cried "no!"

We might have felt ashamed of such compromises, but as children we had no choice. We depended on the adults in our lives for food, shelter, and clothing. Moreover, we were reluctant to give up what little approval we were getting. We had also learned the hard way that asserting ourselves practically guaranteed an onslaught of verbal or physical abuse.

Many of us never outgrew our fear of self-assertion. As adults, our continuing compromises and wishy-washy approach to just about everything caused endless problems in our relationships, in our jobs, and with our own self-image.

Perhaps saddest of all, we didn't give ourselves the chance to build the kind of self-confidence and inner strength that can make life's pathway a smooth and rewarding one.

THOUGHT FOR TODAY: Am I outgrowing my fear of self-assertion?

Self-assertion

November 7

In early recovery, it was extremely encouraging to realize that we were not alone in our fear of self-assertion. The more we identified with the experiences of others, the more hopeful we became that we, too, could overcome our lifelong passivity.

Here are some of the things we learned and gradually put into practice in order to break through our self-imposed restrictions.

With the support of others, we became truly convinced that we had as much right as anyone else to our personal preferences, opinions, and values.

We understood that if we continued to censor our feelings and sublimate our real selves (as we had all our lives), our progress in recovery would be limited.

We became willing to take small risks, putting aside our perennial fear that such actions would bring "punishment." We found that many of the risks we take as adults, even when they don't work out at first, can in the long run be life-enriching.

Little by little, we began to speak up for ourselves, and to take a stand when we felt it was necessary. And slowly but surely, we came into our own.

THOUGHT FOR TODAY: Fear of disapproval will not cause me to hide my true self.

My father and I always had an adversarial relationship. For years I tried to gain his approval and reduce the tension between us, but to no avail.

As time went on and I began to grow spiritually, it became easier for me to be around my father. I was even able to help him in small ways, without expecting anything besides his usual cantankerousness in return.

One day, my father asked me to replace the battery in a smoke alarm. As I was doing so, he shouted insults at me, insisting I was doing it all wrong.

The anger I felt as I climbed down the ladder was all too familiar. But this time, I didn't just take it as I always had. Something came over me—perhaps the beginning of self-respect and inner strength. I told my father, as nonthreateningly as I could, exactly what I thought of his abusive behavior.

He didn't take my criticism well, and soon renewed his attack. At that point, however, his reaction didn't really matter. What did matter was how good my own action made me feel—and what a freeing experience it was to forthrightly state my case.

THOUGHT FOR TODAY: I may be powerless over another person's behavior, but that doesn't prevent me from stating my case.

November 9

The expression "peer pressure" usually refers to the "look-alike, do-alike" influences on young people. As we all know, it can have a dramatic impact on the way youngsters feel about themselves and behave.

We sometimes forget that as adults, we, too, are subjected to all sorts of peer pressure—at work, in the community, among friends. Hardly a day goes by when we're not expected to conform in various ways, or to behave as others behave.

The pressures today may be more subtle than when we were children, but they certainly can be just as overpowering. There's always a temptation to give in and go along—to do what's "expected" so as not to invite disapproval.

But we've come to realize that our self-respect increases in direct relation to our willingness to uphold personal values. So when friends gossip or stand in judgment against a mutual acquaintance, for example, we don't snicker along with them as we once would have.

More seriously, if an employer or associate tries to pressure us into actions that are dishonest or otherwise contrary to our hard-won values, we remember our priorities and stand our ground.

THOUGHT FOR TODAY: Conformity may sometimes be a pressure, but it will never again be a priority.

For some time, a friend had been talking to me about her father. It was obvious from her stories that he was rigid, highly judgmental, and prone to erratic and even violent acts against family members if they "defied" him in some way.

At one point my friend decided to quit college to pursue an acting career. But she didn't tell her father, for fear that he would react explosively and even forbid her from visiting the family home.

"I've lived with that secret for over a year," she told me. "The lies have gotten more and more complicated. My mother and sisters cover up for me just to keep peace with my father.

"But I can't live this way anymore just to stay in his good graces," she continued. "For my own self-respect and peace of mind, I have to tell him the truth."

"You're not afraid?" I asked.

"I am," she answered. "But what he might or might not do isn't the issue anymore. I'm an adult, and I don't have to live by my father's standards, or pretend to. If I can't be my own person and live a life without lies and self-destructive compromises, I'll never get anywhere."

THOUGHT FOR TODAY: I will not live by standards that are not my own.

November 11

Affirmation

I am becoming an individual in my own right. I am developing a solid sense of who I really am, and what I believe and feel. My ideas and opinions are important, and because I'm unafraid to express them and stand behind them, I make a difference.

By asserting myself and taking life-enhancing risks, I am coming into my own. My growing self-confidence and inner strength have smoothed the path, and have made it possible for me to reap the rewards of my bountiful new life.

I am aware that I will always be subjected to the same kinds of negative influences to which everyone else is subjected. Similarly, I will always be powerless over the behavior of others. None of these pressures, however, will prevent me from remaining true to myself, from stating my case, and from standing my ground.

While I may gain outside approval by compromising, or by conforming to other people's standards, I choose not to pay the high price required. Instead, I will continue to assert myself in positive and constructive ways, thereby accruing ever-greater amounts of self-respect and self-esteem.

THOUGHT FOR TODAY: Am I truly aware that my individuality is acceptable—am I free to be me?

46

Love

Love is not getting, but giving; not a wild dream of pleasure, and a madness of desire—oh, no, love is not that—it is goodness, and honor, and peace and pure living.

—Henry Van Dyke

November 12

At the end of my drinking, I was thirty pounds overweight and my skin had a yellowish cast from liver damage. When I spoke to someone, what I said made little sense. For the most part I kept to myself.

I finally reached out for help on a bright summer afternoon. That same evening I was brought together with dozens of recovering alcoholics. I was told that if anyone could help me, they could.

As long as I live, I'll never forget that night. I was half drunk, disheveled, and probably smelled bad, yet those people kept walking up to me. They welcomed me with handshakes and even hugs, and seemed to know exactly how I felt. They encouraged me, offered their help, and told me over and over that everything was going to be all right.

Over the years, I had been to many places and taken many medications to "cure" my alcoholism. But that night, the love I was offered had healing power beyond anything I could have imagined.

It soothed my ragged emotions, took away my pain, let me forget my problems for a few hours, and gave me hope. Best of all, it was freely given and in limitless supply.

THOUGHT FOR TODAY: I will offer my hand to someone in need and remember the healing power of love.

Though we didn't say it aloud, we made it clear through our actions and disposition that our love had to be earned. In fact, the most important word in our vocabulary of love was "if." Our partners, parents, friends, or children could have our love *if* they behaved differently—*if* they made the right choices—*if* they gave us what we wanted.

When we began to live a spiritual life, we learned about an entirely different kind of love—unconditional love—which doesn't depend on anything and has no strings attached.

When we offer unconditional love to someone, we accept that person without reservations or contingencies of any kind; he or she is under no obligation to change in any way. We give our love freely, without the expectation of receiving anything in return.

Though we may aspire to love one another unconditionally, we can never do so completely. For unconditional love is perfect love, and God alone is capable of that. However, as we become less self-centered and acquire greater humility, we are able to remove more and more strings from the love we offer.

THOUGHT FOR TODAY: As we grow spiritually, we're better able to love unconditionally.

November 14

For many years, whenever anyone said "I love you" to me, I would become flustered. I didn't know whether to respond by saying "thank you," by repeating "I love you, too," or by asking "Why?" It was hard for me to believe that anybody could truly feel that way about me.

Love was never expressed and seemed to be rarely felt during my growing-up years. As the result, I didn't have the chance to learn how to give it, how to receive it, or even what love really was. I certainly never learned how to nurture it or build on it.

I know today that the lack of love in my home left me with the feeling that I was unlovable and without much value. I entered adulthood with the conviction that people were basically cold and ungiving.

In early recovery, paradoxically, I relied on other people to convince me that I was deserving of love and capable of loving. Their unwavering acceptance and encouragement spoke volumes about my lovability and value. As time went on, I found ways to "reparent" myself, so to speak—to give myself the love and affection that my parents had been unable to give.

THOUGHT FOR TODAY: I am fully deserving of love.

We used to *worship* other people, putting them up on pedestals while lowering ourselves. We used to *adore* other people, and come up wanting by comparison. We used to *need* other people, because of our own deep sense of insufficiency.

Looking back, our feelings and attitudes toward others were motivated by negative emotions such as fear and envy, rather than by love. Yes, we worshiped, adored, and needed others, but we couldn't really love them because we didn't love ourselves.

Now that we are learning to love ourselves, it's so much easier to relate to others in straightforward rather than self-deprecating ways. Self-love has also changed the way we live our lives day by day.

We have the willingness and desire to take actions that make us feel good about ourselves—not just a small part of ourselves, but our whole selves—not just for the moment, but on a lasting basis.

Our self-love is evident in our willingness to take life-enhancing risks, to be disciplined and hardworking, and to make choices with the potential of elevating rather than diminishing us.

THOUGHT FOR TODAY: The self-love I've begun to feel is based not on egocentricity, but on my genuine worth and equality with others.

Love

November 16

A friend and I were talking about our addictive personalities, and all the things we had grabbed for and become dependent upon to make ourselves whole. "I was hooked on a lot of things over the years," my friend said. "Alcohol, cigarettes, and sugar, to name a few. It turned out I was also addicted to something I didn't even know could *be* addicting—love.

"The only time I felt okay was when I was involved with a man," she continued. "I can't begin to tell you the places I went and the things I did looking for love. But because I was so needy and demanding, none of the relationships ever lasted. I was always disappointed, depressed, and angry.

"I thought lack of love was my problem," my friend went on, "but that wasn't it at all. The problem was the emptiness inside of me—the fact that I'd never really learned to love *myself*. All the men in the world couldn't make up for that.

"In the end I had to treat my addiction to love like any other addiction," she concluded. "I had to admit my powerlessness over it, and then work with God to find a better way to live."

THOUGHT FOR TODAY: The love I've been searching for on the outside can only be found within myself.

True love, the love to which we all aspire, is essentially spiritual in nature. Its flow is more outward than inward. Yet true love is also self-replenishing; it is when we are loving toward another that love grows within ourselves.

We have developed faith, trust, acceptance, honesty, and generosity during our spiritual quest. These qualities have become the expressions of our love today.

For example, when we demonstrate faith by giving a partner or spouse our unqualified support (rather than trying to manage their every move), we are expressing love. When we accept someone exactly as he or she is, including faults, weaknesses, and idiosyncrasies, we are being loving. When we are generous of heart, thinking of others' happiness before our own, we are putting love into action.

We're gradually discovering what love is all about. In the spirit of St. Francis of Assisi's inspiring prayer, we are finding that it is far better to comfort than to be comforted, to understand than to be understood, to give than to receive, to love than to be loved.

THOUGHT FOR TODAY: When I express my love with actions, that is when I feel the most loving.

Love

November 18

Now that I have opened my heart to God, I am experiencing a new kind of love. God's love is unconditional; it is everywhere and ever present; it is never restricted or withheld. I aspire to be loving in those very same ways.

I affirm that I am fully deserving of love and capable of loving others. I will put aside false beliefs along these lines, and take life-enhancing actions to nurture the love within me. If on occasion I have difficulty loving myself, I will remember that God loves me deeply, regardless of how undeserving I may feel.

I have witnessed the healing power of love in my life and the lives of others. That love is abundant within me. Simply by reaching out in the spirit of helpfulness, I can give healing love to another person and perhaps make a difference in his or her life.

As the result of my spiritual growth, I am increasingly able to love others unconditionally. It is becoming possible for me to offer love without the expectation of receiving anything in return, and for that I am most grateful.

THOUGHT FOR TODAY: I can be a channel for God's perfect and abundant love.

Love   368

47

Perspective

There are some minds like either convex or concave mirrors, which represent objects such as they receive them, but they never receive them as they are.

—Joseph Joubert

November 19

We have been making rapid progress in recovering from our dysfunctional past. More is being revealed about the forces that shaped us. We are well on our way toward breaking the chain that has bound us to the emotional limitations of past generations.

But what about our parents? In many cases, they haven't changed at all. They cling to the same old attitudes, behave in the same hurtful ways, and even still try to manipulate us as they did ten, twenty, or thirty years ago.

Thankfully, we've become a lot more understanding and forgiving. Those two qualities, by themselves, go a long way toward helping us deal with these difficult family relationships. We also are learning to keep our parents in perspective, to see them against the backdrop of their own personal histories—to consider the source, and to remind ourselves that they are doing the best they can.

Granted, it's not always easy to be tolerant and compassionate. Sometimes an insensitive act or thoughtless remark can cause us to reflexively revert back to our old ways of reacting. But even then we can quickly recover, so long as we make a sincere effort to regain perspective.

THOUGHT FOR TODAY: Put the problem into perspective. It may not go away, but it will be easier to deal with.

Perspective   370

A friend of mine called to let me know he was going into the hospital. He would be undergoing a surgical procedure known to cause considerable discomfort, as well as a lengthy period of recuperation.

I phoned the day after the surgery and the next day as well. On both occasions my friend complained bitterly about how uncomfortable he was, and about how much work he was missing.

As I set out to visit him at the hospital, I wondered what I might say to cheer him up. It seemed like an impossible challenge, considering that he was overflowing with complaints and self-pity.

When I entered his room he greeted me enthusiastically. He was cheerful, almost ebullient. He apologized for having been so depressed.

"The doctor was in this morning," he said. "He mentioned almost casually how lucky I am. In the past three weeks he had eighteen other patients requiring the same kind of surgery. I was the only one where there were no serious complications, where there wasn't even the hint of malignancy, and where further surgery wasn't necessary. Does that put everything into perspective, or what?"

THOUGHT FOR TODAY: Take the time to compare your troubles with your joys. Put it all into perspective.

Perspective

November 21

From the very first moment that we make a commitment to recovery, remarkable changes begin to occur in our lives. Some take place almost immediately; literally overnight, for example, we find hope and a new sense of direction.

Other changes come about more gradually, in some cases over long periods of time. These longer-term changes can be the most far-reaching of all. A primary case in point is how we gain an entirely new perspective of ourselves in relation to others and the world around us.

In the past, many of us saw ourselves as losers, failures, victims—as nonentities existing on the fringes of society. Today, in miraculous contrast, we see ourselves as part of the whole, as healthy and productive individuals who make a difference.

We once saw others as the main source of our pain and problems. They were always to be feared, and never to be trusted. But we've now come to realize that other people are essential to our continuing recovery. We've come to believe that God Himself works through others, and it follows that today they have become our richest sources of knowledge, comfort, and love.

THOUGHT FOR TODAY: Recovery is enabling me to see myself in ever more accurate perspective.

Perspective   372

Sometimes the most astonishing revelations about ourselves come when we least expect them. Some years ago, for example, a friend and I were browsing through a used car lot and we spotted a 1963 Corvette. "This is the model I worked on!" my friend said excitedly.

I, too, had once worked in an auto assembly plant. It occurred to me that I had a far different perspective of my job than my friend had. I couldn't have cared less about the cars we produced; all I ever thought about was being overworked and underpaid.

The more I thought about it, the more I realized that I approached just about everything in that same way—solely in terms of how it affected *me*. Indeed, most of my life had been warped by a narrow, self-centered perspective.

I viewed other people only in terms of how they might be useful or harmful to me. I certainly didn't consider their feelings or their needs, nor did I see them as individuals with rights, aspirations, and destinies.

Perhaps a seed was planted that day in the used car lot. In any case, my perspective, along with the quality of my life, has changed radically since that time.

THOUGHT FOR TODAY: A self-centered perspective takes more from me than it brings to me.

November 23

We all occasionally lose perspective. As we know, it can be a frightening experience, during which we see things in a distorted and even surrealistic manner. Relatively minor issues loom larger than life, while more serious matters take on earth-shattering proportions.

When we lose perspective, we also tend to lose control of our emotions. We may be filled with fear and confusion, and we're likely to say and do things that we will later regret.

When we temporarily lose touch with reality in this way, how can we regain our emotional balance and once again see things as they really are?

For a moment, we can try to step outside of ourselves and attempt to isolate whatever it was that set us off. We can ask ourselves, "How important is it? Is it worth getting this upset about?"

It can also help to visualize ourselves in relation to the others in our life, to entire nations of people, to the world itself.

One of the best ways to see ourselves and the issues in our life "right size" is to reestablish contact with God. Certain truths will then become evident: We are powerless; God has all power; fundamentally, all is well.

THOUGHT FOR TODAY: Everything relates to something else. Anything can be put into perspective.

As my hard-core atheism gradually gave way to faith and trust in God, many things about me changed dramatically. Perhaps the most profound change was in my perspective—that is to say, in my entire attitude and outlook on life.

During those earlier years when I had mocked the very idea of God, acceptance of life's realities was not my strong suit. Whenever I faced adversity, I would overflow with self-pity and shake my fist at the unfairness of it all.

Now that God is in my life, I see everything with different eyes. I've come to believe that there is a plan and purpose for all that takes place—that each occurrence and even each seeming adversity has its place in the larger order.

Faith in God's will has helped me put my own will into perspective. I no longer have to fight everything and everybody to get my way. I may not always understand why things happen as they do, but I am willing to try to understand that it is for the greater good, as God sees that greater good.

THOUGHT FOR TODAY: My new perspective is born of faith, not of fear.

November 25

Affirmation

Today I gratefully acknowledge the change in perspective that I have undergone during my years of recovery. Never in my life have I been more comfortable within myself and with those around me.

With a true perspective, I can more easily accept and deal with life's ongoing challenges. When I face serious problems, I can find solace by counterbalancing them with the many blessings in my life.

When it is necessary for me to be involved with difficult people, I will try to take the time to consider their personal histories and individual backgrounds. The perspective I am likely to gain in each case can help me to be more understanding and tolerant.

If I temporarily lose perspective, I will try to remember that it is not necessary for me to suffer long in that state. I need only draw closer to God, once again affirming my relative lack of power and His all-encompassing power. I need only remind myself that God loves me—that He has faith in my ability to meet the challenges and seize the opportunities He places before me each day.

THOUGHT FOR TODAY: Perspective is more than just a way of looking at things. It can be a tool for living.

48

Faith

We have but faith: we cannot know,
* For knowledge is of things we see;*
* And yet we trust it comes from Thee,*
A beam in darkness: let it grow.

— ALFRED TENNYSON

November 26

Because our faith in a Higher Power is personal, individual, and even mysterious, it is difficult to describe and impossible to measure. But our faith can always be strengthened, even though it cannot be quantified.

In my own case, my faith has been strengthened as the result of a variety of actions, experiences, and realizations over the years. At times I purposely set out to deepen my faith; on many other occasions it has been enhanced through events and insights that have come my way unexpectedly.

My faith is strengthened when I think about my life—what it used to be like, how it has changed, and what it's like today. There's no doubt in my mind that the transformation would not have taken place without the power and grace of God.

My faith is strengthened when I pray, and then see evidence that my prayers have been answered.

My faith is strengthened when I interact with other recovering people, and I can see the miracle of God's healing take place before my eyes.

My faith is strengthened whenever I become intellectually and emotionally involved with nature. Then I see God everywhere.

THOUGHT FOR TODAY: Each time I express gratitude to God, my faith deepens.

When calamities occur in our lives, we find comfort and reassurance by reaching out to God. In periods of dire need, our faith usually grows stronger.

There are times, however, when some of us begin to question our faith. The trigger may be a personal tragedy. Or perhaps our faith is shaken by a natural disaster in which many lives have been lost.

We feel that God has let us down. We become confused, and angry at Him. We may feel that we've been deceived by God, or that we've deceived ourselves by placing so much faith in Him in the first place. One way or another, we find ourselves in an emotional maelstrom.

When the turbulence subsides and we come back to our senses, we may then turn on ourselves in a different way. We may feel guilty for "betraying" our Higher Power by temporarily losing faith.

At such times, we need to remember that we are not saints—that our faltering faith is a reflection of our humanness. We also need to remind ourselves that while our faith may occasionally fluctuate, God's love for us is constant and unwavering.

THOUGHT FOR TODAY: If my faith temporarily falters, I will not judge myself harshly.

November 28

When we ventured forth with even the barest beginnings of faith, beneficial results were soon evident in our lives. As our faith has deepened over the years, a great deal more has been added.

Faith in God makes it possible for us to more easily accept unfolding events, including seeming adversity, and to view whatever happens as part of an overall flow of ultimate good. We no longer need to torment ourselves by analyzing and dissecting each new reality in terms of negative or positive, pro or con, failure or success.

Faith is responsible for most of our inner changes. For years we tried and were unable to change on our own. We have since learned that God has the power to remove our obsessions, compulsions, and character flaws. All we need do is find the willingness and humility to ask for His help.

We find that faith is part of the solution to virtually every problem and dilemma that surfaces. When we are anchored in faith, we are always able to regain our emotional stability. Faith brings us peace of mind.

THOUGHT FOR TODAY: Faith has given us freedoms that were previously not attainable—freedom from anger, anxiety, and fear.

Just because we are in recovery, that doesn't mean everything is going to go smoothly from now on. Life is still in session. It's inevitable that from time to time we'll find ourselves facing an unexpected setback or formidable new challenge.

When we are in this position, it's frequently difficult to know what to do, to get what we think we need to solve the problem, or to find a way out. But no matter how tumultuous the circumstances or distraught our feelings, it is always possible for us to find the answers—and, eventually, serenity—in faith.

We can begin generating that faith by seeking out a quiet place within ourselves. We can then center our thoughts on God's presence and power in our lives. We can remind ourselves of the previous times God has seen us through. And we can reaffirm the truth that He is more powerful than any set of physical symptoms, financial setbacks, or perplexing circumstances.

As faith grows within us, we may be guided toward actual solutions to our problem, or we may simply become willing to follow our intuition. In either case, we find the courage to move forward.

THOUGHT FOR TODAY: The more I affirm my faith, the stronger it becomes, and the more effectively I can act in faith.

November 30

After many years in an unhappy marriage, a woman decided to file for divorce. It had become clear that the relationship was beyond repair, so she committed herself to doing what was necessary to restructure her life and start anew.

During the next several months, the woman spent a great deal of time preparing herself. Once she had chosen a lawyer, she carefully reviewed her financial situation and future prospects. She explored career-training possibilities and contacted several schools.

The woman also decided where to live following the divorce, and began looking for a place. She brought her two grown children together and talked things out with them.

"The most important thing I did during that whole painful time," she says, "was to stay in touch with God and constantly reaffirm my faith in Him." She knew she would have to rely on God to see her through the days of uncertainty and emotional turmoil that she would likely face.

"When I finally felt ready to put my plans into motion," the woman says, "it was my faith, above all else, that lightened my load and made it possible to move forward in spite of my fear."

THOUGHT FOR TODAY: With faith in God and myself, I can confidently face what is in front of me.

Faith   382

Faith is described in the Scriptures as "the assurance of things hoped for, the conviction of things not seen." Faith may not be visible, but it can be the rock of our being.

We cannot look ahead and see the future, but we have faith that God knows what is in store for us. He prepares us each day for what lies ahead. We feel secure when we place ourselves in His care, for we are confident that He is leading us toward a personal destiny that is good and right for us.

We have the solid inner conviction that God's love is present and at work in all our affairs. This knowledge enables us to face each day fearlessly and with positive anticipation, and to direct our thoughts and actions along constructive lines.

We try to meet each turn of events with an active and dynamic faith. Whatever we are asked to do, whatever choices we have to make, we ask God for help, and then go forth with assurance that all will be well.

THOUGHT FOR TODAY: Faith is the lodestar within. Its revealing light penetrates confusion and brightens the road ahead.

December 2

Affirmation

As time goes on, I am increasingly aware of God's presence. I see unmistakable evidence of His miracles within me and around me, and my faith deepens with each new day.

Faith has brought great abundance to my life. The knowledge that there is an all-powerful guiding force has given me the ability to accept changes in the outside world, and to experience positive changes within myself that otherwise would not have been possible.

Faith gives me the confidence to go forward even when I don't see the road ahead, or can't understand why I am being led in a particular direction.

When I turn to God in faith, I am provided with peace of mind and a sense of well-being, no matter what the situation or circumstance. Even when my emotions are awry and my thoughts are confused, I can count on faith to anchor and stabilize me.

As I use material resources, they tend to diminish in effectiveness and eventually lose their value. When I put my faith into practice, however, it grows stronger. The more I apply and depend on faith, the more faith I have.

THOUGHT FOR TODAY: With abiding faith, I place myself in God's hands.

49

Trust

Those who trust us, educate us.
—George Eliot

December 3

As children in dysfunctional families, we developed many misguided beliefs. Few of them were more deeply ingrained and longer-lasting than the conviction that people were not to be trusted.

And why wouldn't we feel that way? The truth was that we rarely could count on anybody; getting close and becoming vulnerable usually meant being betrayed and hurt. If we told our family members how we felt about certain things, for example, they either didn't understand, or would use our confidences against us in some way later on.

As adults, we expected the widening circle of people in our lives to be just as undependable as our parents had been. We believed that the past would repeat itself, that our security depended on remaining closed up and ever cautious, that our anger at all the world's untrustworthy people was totally justified.

We eventually began to understand that the painful feelings we retained as adults resulted not from what people did or said, but from our reactions to those words and deeds. Moreover, we realized that if we didn't change our way of thinking, we would remain fearful and alienated for the rest of our lives.

THOUGHT FOR TODAY: Is my belief that people can't be trusted still causing me pain?

We don't like to dwell on the past, and are fond of saying such things as, "That was then, and this is now." Occasionally, however, we find it helpful to think about the past in order to review the progress we've made over the months and years. Our growing trust of others is a case in point, and can usually provide us with the dramatic contrast we need.

In the past we lived in a small world, closed in by limiting beliefs and negative attitudes. Today, our ability to trust is breaking down the barriers between our world and the larger world, and between ourselves and others.

In the past, we were always on edge and on guard, fearful of being betrayed or injured in some way. Today, we are far more at ease around people because we trust them—and we're finally free to be ourselves.

In the past, our lack of trust allowed us to harbor and nurture resentments—to be unforgiving and even vengeful. Today, when a person lets us down, we're less likely to take it personally. We're more accepting, and better able to see a broken promise as simply part of someone's humanness.

THOUGHT FOR TODAY: My growing trust in others is bringing about a myriad of positive changes in my life.

December 5

I used to carry around a grab bag of cynical phrases applicable to just about any situation. Among my favorites was this one: "I trust him just about as far as I can throw him."

To put it mildly, I was not a trusting soul. I had come to believe that putting one's faith in others brought only disappointment and pain.

Learning to trust was one of my greatest challenges in recovery. As I recall, the turnaround began with a gradual willingness to take small risks. I tried, for example, to become receptive to the support and encouragement that was offered ceaselessly by new-found friends.

After a few months, I singled out several people with whom I felt safe in sharing my feelings and fears. I was drawn to men and women who didn't gossip, who seemed to accept me as I was, and who "walked like they talked."

Eventually, I became completely trusting of one man in particular. I was able to tell him secrets about myself I thought I would take to the grave. That experience was an enormous breakthrough for me, which in time led to trusting relationships with more and more of my new friends.

THOUGHT FOR TODAY: I can't flourish in recovery unless I learn to trust my fellows.

Trust   388

For a long time, many of us didn't differentiate between faith in God and trust in Him. We knew that our faith was a potent spiritual force within us, and that it worked. Our experience showed us that God was capable of bringing about seemingly miraculous changes in our lives and the lives of others.

Over time, we realized that trust goes even further than faith. As we've come to understand it, trust is putting faith into action through prayer and meditation. When we trust in God, we fully rely on His wisdom, guidance, and strength to carry us through the unfolding challenges of each new day.

We try to react to the uncertainties that will always be part of life by placing our fears and doubts in His hands. It's so much easier to get through painful and unforeseen circumstances that way.

Today we are confident that God has our best interests in mind at all times—that He knows what is right for us in all respects and in all situations. Because of our trust in Him, we have inner certainty that He has a perfect plan for our lives no matter what is taking place around us.

THOUGHT FOR TODAY: I trust that God's plan for my life is far better than any I could possibly conceive on my own.

December 7

Today I trust myself. I rarely think about it, but when I do, it gives me a solid feeling.

When I need to make a decision and the choices aren't clear-cut, I can rely on my intuition. When I make a commitment, I can trust myself to keep it. When I'm talking with someone, I don't have to worry about saying the wrong thing.

There was a time when I couldn't trust myself at all. Because of my moodiness and impulsiveness, I never knew what I might say or do. I had no idea who I really was, so I couldn't develop firm opinions, let alone trust them. My self-centered wants were so overpowering that they blocked out whatever objectivity and intuition I may have had.

Self-trust hasn't been a conscious goal in recovery, but has flowed out of other changes that have taken place. As I've become more self-aware and taken steps to shed my character flaws, my erratic behavior has improved. I've become more responsible to myself and others, and am better able to finish what I start. I've begun to know, deep down, that my motives have changed—that I can trust my feelings, thoughts, and actions.

THOUGHT FOR TODAY: Now that I'm living a spiritual life, I can trust my inner voice.

I once asked a friend to house-sit for me while I was on vacation. He quickly agreed, and told me that he had helped others in the same way several times before. Once, he said, he was left in charge of a ranch with dogs, cats, chickens, parrots, and horses.

"I really like house-sitting," he said. "Besides the money, it makes for a nice change in routine. Most of all, I like the feeling of being trusted."

Some years earlier, people wouldn't have dreamed of asking him to look after their property. He was so irresponsible and *un*trustworthy, he recalled, that his neighbors wouldn't so much as lend him a screwdriver.

"Once you let someone trust you," he said proudly, "that means you've made a commitment to live up to that trust. But people don't just start trusting you automatically. You have to open the door to trust, and then you have to earn it.

"I've tried to do a lot of things over the years to boost my self-esteem," he added. "But being trustworthy—not just physically, but emotionally and financially, too—that's done more than anything to help me feel good about myself."

THOUGHT FOR TODAY: Can my friends count on me the way I can count on them?

December 9

Affirmation

Because of my growing trust in myself, in others and in God, I am unafraid to experience life whole-heartedly. I am becoming ever more comfortable in the world, and am increasingly certain that I will be able to face and deal with whatever is put in my path.

Trust in myself allows me to explore and develop my inner resources, and to express and stand by my opinions. Self-trust also allows me to rely on my intuition, to have confidence in my choices, and to take the risks that move me forward.

Trust in others breaks down the barriers that once kept me alienated and alone. I have discovered that my fellows have rich resources of experience, strength, and hope; as long as I remain trusting, those resources are freely available to me.

Trust in God has all but eliminated the phrases, "Not again!" and "Why me?" from my vocabulary. I have deep and abiding confidence that He has a perfect design for my life. No matter where I go, what I attempt, or what occurs, trust in Him brings me serenity, security, and a sense of wholeness.

THOUGHT FOR TODAY: Trust brings new dimensions to living, loving, and learning.

50

Choices

What is freedom? Freedom is the right to choose: the right to create for yourself the alternatives of choice. Without the possibility of choice and the exercise of choice a man is not a man but a member, an instrument, a thing.

—ARCHIBALD MACLEISH

December 10

There was a lengthy period of time in our lives when we lacked freedom of choice. Practically everything we did we had to do. There were no options and alternatives, or so it seemed.

We may have been chemically or behaviorally dependent, and deprived of choice by our addictions. Our own damaged emotions may have blinded us to choices, or perhaps fear caused us to abdicate decision-making to others.

In recovery, all of that has changed. Self-discovery, acceptance, and spiritual strength have made us aware of choices we never knew we had, and given us the capability of making them.

Today we are deeply grateful for the choices we have in virtually every area. When we arise each morning, we can freely choose how to approach the day. For the most part we can determine our attitude as well as our behavior—how we respond to the day's events, and how we interact with others.

Best of all, we have important choices concerning the way we see ourselves, the way we feel about ourselves, and the way we treat ourselves. We are no longer on a one-way street.

THOUGHT FOR TODAY: Freedom from fear gives me freedom of choice.

When we were youngsters in dysfunctional homes, there were lines not meant to be crossed and words not meant to be spoken. We were expected to go along, to be seen but not heard, to behave in a certain manner. We were allowed very few choices.

We have since come into our own as adults. As a result, it is becoming increasingly easy to make the right choices concerning family matters. In the first place, we are free to decide just how involved we're willing to be with various family members. Now that we've become self-aware and emotionally stable, such choices are relatively painless to make.

Moreover, we can forthrightly choose not to go along with behavior that is harmful to us or others. We can choose not to play the same old deadly games, or to slip back into roles we were forced to play as children.

Today we can choose to be our own person, to honor truth rather than succumb to falsehood, to state our case and maintain our integrity. We can draw our own lines and establish our own limits.

THOUGHT FOR TODAY: My only limitations are those that I impose on myself.

December 12

As a recovering alcoholic, the most important choice I make each day is not to take the first drink, pill, or other mind-altering chemical. The fact that I even have such a choice is a miracle.

Now that I have been restored to sobriety and sanity, I am fully capable of making the choice. Moreover, I know exactly how to make it, and I am sharply aware of what will happen if I don't make it.

I approach my sobriety a day at a time, choosing each morning to stay clean and sober. I begin the day by putting my priorities in order, reminding myself that I am powerless over alcohol, and that for me to drink is to die. I ask God to help me stay sober.

I know well from past experience what will happen if I take my sobriety for granted and make the wrong choice. By picking up the first drink or pill, I might as well plead guilty—no matter what the charge. I give up all my dignity, all my self-respect, all my rights as a person. I give up *all* my choices.

THOUGHT FOR TODAY: I choose sobriety and soundness of mind.

Most of us dread making decisions. When we stop to think about it, however, our inner turmoil comes more from *not* making them, than from actually committing ourselves one way or the other. Yet there are actions we can take to help us become more decisive and make choices more easily.

When we face the need to make a difficult decision, it's always a good idea to find out as much as we can about the subject at hand—whether it involves buying a car, accepting a job offer, or setting up a timetable.

From there, we can list all the pros and cons and, as honestly as we're able, weigh one side against the other. It's usually helpful at that point to discuss the matter with someone whose judgment and objectivity we respect.

Many of us have found that the most beneficial step we can take, by far, is to ask for God's wisdom and guidance in arriving at the proper decision.

It's important to remember that decisions are not necessarily etched in stone and irrevocable once we make them. Most decisions can be modified or even reversed as changing circumstances dictate.

THOUGHT FOR TODAY: My best decision is the one that gets me off the fence of indecision.

December 14

After we had spent an hour at a wedding reception, I noticed that my friend had a forlorn expression. I turned to her and asked, "What's the matter?
Why do you look so sad?"

"I can't help it," she answered tersely, effectively
blocking any further inquiry on my part.

After a moment, my friend backtracked apologet-
ically. "I told you I can't help it, but that's simply not
true. I *can* help it. I *can* help looking sad and feeling
sad, and I'm going to try to get out of my funk.

"The thing is," she went on, "I used to use those
four words constantly. 'I can't help it'—that was my
automatic response to any question having to do with
my feelings or my conduct. And in a sense it was true.
Either I really couldn't help the way I was acting, or
I used the phrase as an excuse.

"It's getting to be a lot different today," my friend
concluded. "I can help myself if I *choose* to. I know
what I can and can't do, and most of the time I'm
willing to put forth the effort. So now, let's get back to
your question. . . ."

THOUGHT FOR TODAY: Thankfully, I now have
clear choices concerning my attitude and behavior.

Today we cherish life and have growing respect for ourselves and our place in the world. Now that we feel this way, it has become important to make the right choices concerning our physical, emotional, and spiritual well-being.

When we don't attend to our physical needs, our thinking tends to go off the track and even become destructive. That's why we choose to devote time and energy to exercising, eating right, and getting enough rest and recreation.

In the same way, now that we are aware of what's healthful for us emotionally, it's a lot easier to make the right choices in that area. Because of our positive feelings for ourselves, we reserve the right to privacy, the right to say 'no,' and the right to choose the company we keep.

Reverence for life and self-respect has also heightened our desire to grow spiritually. We have chosen to regularly set aside time for communication with our Higher Power, seeking to know His will for us. Through prayer and meditation, as well as such other activities as nature walks and retreats, we strive to replenish ourselves spiritually.

THOUGHT FOR TODAY: My spiritual, emotional, and physical well-being depends on the choices I make and the actions I take each day.

December 16

Affirmation

My freedom of choice is among my hardest-won and most precious assets. In order to acquire it, I first had to build self-awareness and self-confidence. I had to do a lot of growing up.

Today I'm willing to do whatever is necessary to preserve my power of choice. I will not abdicate it to anyone or anything, including individuals, jobs, or mind-altering substances.

My willingness and ability to make healthy choices has done wonders for my self-esteem. I can gauge my progress in recovery by the choices I make. As an important example, I choose relationships that are mutually respectful and beneficial; I choose to avoid or end relationships that are degrading and harmful.

I will remember that my power of choice does not give me license to run roughshod over the feelings of others. I will try to be sensitive and understanding of the needs of family members, friends, and coworkers even while I make the choices necessary for my continued well-being.

My personal choices today are myriad. They encompass my attitude and perspective, my reactions and interactions, the way I feel about myself, and the way I treat myself.

THOUGHT FOR TODAY: Now that I have freedom of choice, it is my responsibility to use it in the best way possible.

Choices   400

51

Serenity

Peace does not dwell in outward things, but within the soul; we may preserve it in the midst of the bitterest pain, if our will remain firm and submissive. Peace in this life springs from acquiescence, not in an exemption from suffering.

—François de S. Fénelon

December 17

There must have been times in my old life when I felt really serene, but in all honesty I can't remember more than a few such occasions. When I think about those days, I am brought back to the fear I felt growing up, the high anxiety that characterized my seven-day-a-week drinking, and the constant tension and turmoil at home and at work.

My life isn't the least bit like that anymore. While it's true that I occasionally go through periods of fear, anxiety, and stress, most of the time I have a true sense of well-being. There are no fires to put out, no excuses to be invented, nobody chasing me for any reason. Day after day, with few exceptions, I am at peace with myself.

I cherish the serenity I have. It's important for me to remember, however, that it didn't come to me out of the blue, nor will it stay with me automatically and forever. Serenity is the direct result of the way I live my life today—the values I honor, the principles I practice, the choices I make, the actions I take.

THOUGHT FOR TODAY: Serenity or stress—most of the time I do have a choice.

We pass a friend in the hallway at work. He rolls his eyes and mutters, "I should have stayed in bed." We nod sympathetically; we all have days like that.

Nothing goes right. No matter what we do or how hard we try, everything unravels. Our own brain-chatter makes it even worse. The volume in our head is turned way up, we're scanning six different stations, and a committee of insane DJs is criticizing every move we make.

How can we put a stop to the madness? It may seem that serenity is light-years away, yet there are definite actions we can take to quickly bring it back.

Probably the first thing we need to do is "turn off our head," by phoning or taking aside a close friend and describing exactly what we're feeling. A simple act like that can usually shut down even the most garrulous committee.

Next, we can put our priorities in order, mapping out a simple plan of action, then identifying and letting go of responsibilities that are not ours. Finally, once we've begun to slow down, we can step gently back into reality and start over, putting one foot in front of the other.

THOUGHT FOR TODAY: The "committee" in my head may be unreal, but it can do real damage.

December 19

Serenity is something we each experience in a personal way. There is one fact, however, on which we all agree: Our individual serenity, or lack of it, relates directly to the way we practice the spiritual principles we have come to value.

For example, we are far more likely to have continuing peace of mind when we are rigorously honest in all we say or do, than when we try to slip by with half-truths or exaggeration.

In the same way, serenity is always closer at hand when we remain self-aware—by staying in touch with our feelings rather than letting them eat away at us. We're also more likely to be at peace when we talk openly about our concerns and problems, instead of keeping them bottled up.

To gain and maintain serenity, we need to take care of unfinished business each day. For example, if we are wrong, we promptly admit it; if we've had a misunderstanding, we clear the air.

And finally, there can be no disagreement about the vital connection between serenity and acceptance. The better able we are to accept ourselves and others, the greater our peace of mind.

THOUGHT FOR TODAY: Am I doing what it takes to gain and maintain serenity?

Our lives were in constant chaos. At home, at work—even on vacation—we would bounce out of one crisis right into another. Something always needed to be worked out, taken care of, looked after.

Then there were the really bad days, when we'd step out of bed right into an endless mine field. No matter how careful we were, every few hours another hidden booby-trap would explode and send us sky-high.

It all began to change for the better when we gained enough self-honesty to ask ourselves a series of probing questions:

Didn't we often turn minor mishaps into big deals to get a rush of self-importance? Didn't we feel bored or empty when we *weren't* neck-deep in a crisis? In truth, hadn't we been hooked on adrenaline for most of our lives?

And what about those explosions? Weren't they completely of our own making? Wasn't it time to stop tiptoeing through the mine fields? In fact, wasn't it time to stop planting the mines in the first place? Weren't we ready to finally start living a peaceful life?

THOUGHT FOR TODAY: I will initiate calm, rather than instigate chaos.

December 21

We have come to believe that the peace of mind we enjoy in our lives today is a direct outgrowth of our relationship with God. In a world of ongoing and sometimes bewildering change, there is one constant on which we can depend: We are never alone, for God is always with us.

Thoughts of God fill us with a sense of inner peace. We know from direct experience that His love can free us from stress, anxiety, and negative attitudes. All we have to do is ask.

If at any time we become fearful or confused, we can turn within to reestablish contact with God's love. It is there, in the silence, that we can find peace. We can then move forward and face any situation, any responsibility, any challenge, with confidence and poise.

Our awareness of God's presence reassures us that He is guiding us toward all that is right and good for our lives. And we become serene. Our awareness of God's healing and strengthening power gives us confidence that all is well. And we remain serene.

THOUGHT FOR TODAY: My consciousness of God is the ultimate source of serenity.

Some time ago, a friend and I went lake fishing. Although she had never fished before, my friend quickly learned to use a rod and reel. Unfortunately, however, the fish weren't biting. After sitting for three hours without so much as a nibble, I thanked her for being a good sport.

"No, this is great," she said, "just being out here on the water. But I'll tell you, a year or so ago it would have been impossible for me to sit still this long."

She went on to say that she used to envy people who could relax, do nothing, and still be at peace. She believed that she was physiologically incapable of that kind of tranquility, because she was too high-strung and hyperactive.

"It wasn't until last year that I realized why I was so uncomfortable during idle moments," my friend explained. "The culprit wasn't my body, but my mind. It was always blasting away at me—with guilt, criticism, whatever. If I kept busy, I was a moving target, and harder to hit.

"Just understanding that was enough to reverse a lifelong pattern," she concluded. "My mind doesn't have anywhere near the negative power it used to. I'm finally learning to relax."

THOUGHT FOR TODAY: I can be alone; I can be relaxed and comfortable with myself.

December 23

Affirmation

I cherish the serenity I have in my life today, and I will do what is necessary to gain and maintain continuing peace of mind.

Calmness or chaos: The choice is mine. I choose to let go of responsibilities that belong to others. I choose not to worry needlessly about matters that are beyond my control. I choose not to pressure myself by blowing things out of proportion.

I no longer need to fill my days with confusion and crises in order to avoid dealing with hidden feelings. I'm so grateful that I have learned to enjoy tranquility, that I can be comfortable and relaxed when I am alone.

I resolve not to take my serenity for granted. Each day, I will take actions that I know will bring me inner peace. I will be as self-honest as possible, staying in touch with my feelings and talking about them when necessary. I will strive to be ever more accepting of myself and the world around me.

Above all else, I will find serenity through dependence on God. No matter what, His love can always bring me inner calm.

THOUGHT FOR TODAY: My serenity is centered in spirituality.

52

Fellowship

There is a destiny that makes us brothers, none goes his way alone. All that we send into the lives of others comes back into our own.

—EDWIN MARKHAM

December 24

Because of my upbringing, the ability to care about other people didn't come naturally to me. On those occasions when I did want to reach out in a loving way, it was all but impossible for me to follow through. I was too self-conscious, too fearful, or I simply didn't know how to put my feelings into words and actions.

Only in recovery, through the chemistry of fellowship, did I finally understand how natural it could be to care about others and allow them to care for me.

For the first time I had the feeling—indeed, the proof—that other people genuinely cared about my welfare, my state of mind, and my progress. Their empathy and unwavering loyalty made it possible for me to carry on even when I was tempted to back off or run away.

On the other side of the coin, the more deeply involved in fellowship I became, the easier it was for me to reach out to others. I soon began to really care about their concerns, their well-being, their progress in recovery. How good it made me feel about myself when I was able to have those feelings about others.

THOUGHT FOR TODAY: Through fellowship, we love each other back to health.

When we first witnessed people sharing their innermost feelings at a group level, it was all that some of us could do to keep from squirming. We were uncomfortable for several reasons. In the first place, we didn't think it was proper for people to air their "dirty laundry" that way. And second, we had been taught not only to keep our problems to ourselves, but to handle them ourselves. To act otherwise was to be an embarrassment.

Within a short time, however, we were captivated by the honesty of the sharing as well as the spirited support it evoked. When people had the courage to open up in front of others, it seemed to give their recovery an almost tangible new dimension.

By sharing, they were able to unburden themselves and experience relief. Moreover, they often received encouraging feedback from the group, as well as specific suggestions from those who had undergone similar experiences. And finally, the sharing and interchanges seemed to prove helpful even to those who were simply listening.

In my own case, I was at first reluctant to share honestly at a group level—primarily because of my need to look good. Once I was able to begin opening up, however, embarrassment gave way to exhilaration and new hope.

THOUGHT FOR TODAY: Fellowship encourages openness; openness encourages healing.

December 26

Thousands upon thousands of us each felt that we were different from everyone else. We didn't fit in—we never had and never would. Our problems were unique, and most likely unsolvable. We felt alienated and out of sync.

When we gradually came into contact with each other through ever-widening circles of fellowship, we were relieved to discover that the feelings we believed were so unique to each of us were, in reality, common to all of us.

What a pleasant jolt it was to discover how well our new friends understood us—*really* understood us—even though we had just met and were practically strangers. They knew not only what we were feeling when we were feeling it, but why we had the feeling. They could quickly tell that we were insecure and threatened, for example, because they frequently had been in that same emotional cul-de-sac themselves.

As we became more self-aware, we, too, were able to recognize ourselves in the feelings and actions of others. And because of our ability to identify at such deep levels, no matter where we go we usually feel a sense of fellowship and belonging—rather than alienation and loneliness.

THOUGHT FOR TODAY: To the extent that I know myself, I can know others. To the extent that I love myself, I can love others.

Fellowship   412

When everything seems to be going wrong, and my emotions grow ragged, I sometimes convince myself that being around other people is the last thing in the world I need. I feel vulnerable, even fragile; I think I need to be alone in order to solve my problems. Besides, I tell myself, nobody would really understand.

When I isolate myself and turn my back on fellowship, I invariably become more confused. I lose touch with my spiritual self, and with the principles that have been fundamental to my progress thus far. My thinking and behavior during these periods of isolation serve to intensify the emotional pain that drove me to seclusion in the first place.

Sometimes I have to suffer by myself and go to the end of the line, so to speak, before I ask for help. At other times I don't choose to wait that long; I pick up the phone and tell a friend what's going on. When I share my problems, and my feelings about them, I almost always receive what I need from my fellows: Wisdom, support, and love.

THOUGHT FOR TODAY: Isolation will compound my problems; fellowship can help to alleviate them.

Fellowship

December 28

In our relationships with others, we tended in the past to think and act in extremes. At times, for example, we completely shunned our friends and loved ones as a way to display our alleged independence. At other times we were overly dependent and, because of our neediness, literally squeezed dry those very same people.

Thankfully, we've since achieved a degree of emotional stability and settled into a middle ground called interdependence. Our close friendships are now based on mutual trust and caring. If we have a primary goal in these relationships today, it is to help each other grow emotionally and spiritually in order to fulfill our individual potentials in the best possible way.

What kinds of relationships do we value most today? They are those in which we unreservedly give the best within ourselves to each other, without expecting or demanding anything in return—least of all control over one another. Our healthy interdependence enables us to freely work out and exchange solutions with each other, to appraise as well as praise, and to clearly and accurately see ourselves through the eyes of loving friends.

THOUGHT FOR TODAY: Am I seeking the healthy middle ground of interdependence in my relationships today?

At a recovery group discussion a while ago, I shared some experiences I had with "judgmentalism." As I recall, I made two points. First, the qualities I find offensive in others are often the very same qualities I dislike in myself. Second, the more judgmental I am, the more angry and uncomfortable I become, because my judgmentalism creates a hostile environment in and around me.

Later, a young man told me how much he identified with what I had said. It was the first time he had been able to see how much his own judgmentalism had been hurting him, and why.

I was momentarily tempted to take credit for enlightening him. But I reminded myself that my thoughts were hardly original; they had been passed on to me in exactly the same way.

Indeed, most of what I have learned about myself over the years has come not from some wellspring of innate wisdom, but from other people who freely shared what had been given to them. That's one of the main reasons I continue to seek fellowship with other recovering people—so I can continue to identify with their experience, and in the process understand more about myself.

THOUGHT FOR TODAY: Fellowship is often a shortcut to self-awareness.

December 30

On the surface, even somewhat below the surface, it seems at first that we are as different from one another as people can be. We are of different ages and sexes, political and religious affiliations, careers and economic levels, colors and creeds.

But when we probe a little deeper and get to know each other better, we find startling similarities.

We each have been through some kind of personal hell. In many ways, our feelings are identical. We have overriding common goals—to be relieved of our obsessions, to get well, to turn our lives around. We are travelers, journeying from different places, yet all merging onto the same path of spirituality.

Our unique bonds bring about a mutual, almost unconditional acceptance of one another. We are encouraged to freely share problems, fears, and hopes, both past and present. We are offered guidance on how to remain on our new path, but never mandated to do so.

We are given attention and consideration; we are taken seriously no matter what we say or do. We are never scrutinized or shunned, never ridiculed or mocked. We are always welcomed by our fellows.

THOUGHT FOR TODAY: I can strengthen the bonds with my fellows by focusing on our similarities rather than our differences.

Affirmation

Today I give thanks for the decisive role fellowship continues to play in my life. Because of the close personal bonds I have with others who share a desire to grow spiritually, my recovery has taken on new dimensions.

Through fellowship, I am offered a wealth of experience, strength, and hope. Identification with my new friends leads me to greater self-awareness. The better I understand myself, the easier it becomes to discover and discard my character flaws.

Fellowship allows me to see myself through the eyes of others. My friends sometimes recognize positive qualities I never knew I had. They see change and growth when I may not yet be able to, and they guide me back on course when I occasionally take a wrong turn.

Now I have a sense of belonging, where before I felt alienation and loneliness. Now I focus gladly on similarities, where before I could see only differences.

Perhaps the greatest blessing of fellowship is the unique acceptance we have for one another. It flows from our common suffering, our common goals, and our common desire to draw closer to our Creator.

THOUGHT FOR TODAY: By encouraging honesty and openness, fellowship accelerates my recovery.